SKINNY SEAFOOD

by BARBARA GRUNES

Surrey Books
CHICAGO, ILLINOIS 60611

SKINNY SEAFOOD is published by Surrey Books, Inc.,
230 E. Ohio St., Suite 120, Chicago, IL 60611.

First edition: 1 2 3 4 5

This book is manufactured in the United States of America.

Library of Congress Cataloging-in-Publication data:

Grunes, Barbara.
    Skinny seafood / by Barbara Grunes. – 1st ed.
        170   p.   cm.
    Includes index.
    ISBN 0–940625–59–8 : $20.95. – ISBN 0–940625–58–X (pbk.): $12.95
    1. Cookery (Seafood) 2. Low-fat diet–Recipes.   3. Low-calorie
diet–Recipes. I. Title.
TX747.G837 1993
641.6'92–dc20   92–46086
                                                              CIP

Editorial and production: *Bookcrafters, Inc., Chicago*
Nutritional analyses: *Linda R. Yoakum, M.S., R.D.*
Art direction: *Hughes & Co., Chicago*
Cover and interior illustrations by *Laurel DiGangi*
Back of cover photos, courtesy *California Olive Industry*

For free catalog and prices on quantity purchases, contact Surrey Books at the
address above.

This title is distributed to the trade by Publishers Group West.

Other Titles in the "Skinny" Cookbooks Series:

Skinny Pizzas
Skinny Soups
Skinny Spices
Skinny Beef (fall, 1993)
Skinny Cakes, Cookies, and Sweets (fall, 1993)
Skinny Potatoes (fall, 1993)

CONTENTS

Nutrition Data for Popular Seafood

Fish (3-oz. portion)	Cal- ories	Pro- tein (gm)	Fat (gm)	Choles- terol (mg)	So- dium (mg)	Sat. Fat (gm)	% Cal. Fat
Bass	82	15.8	1.7	35	58	0.4	20
Catfish	99	15.4	3.6	49	54	0.8	35
Clams (canned)	125	21.7	1.7	57	95	0.2	12
Clams (fresh)	63	10.9	0.8	29	48	0.1	12
Cod	64	14.0	0.5	34	48	0.1	8
Crab	83	16.3	1.4	81	225	0.2	16
Finnan Haddie (smoked haddock)	99	21.4	0.8	65	649	0.1	8
Flounder	77	16.0	1.0	45	69	0.2	12
Grouper	78	16.4	0.9	31	35	0.2	11
Haddock	74	16.1	0.6	49	58	0.1	8
Halibut	93	17.7	1.9	27	46	0.3	20
King Crab (with shell)	21	4.1	0.3	11	228	0.0	15
Lobster	83	17.4	0.5	61	323	0.1	6
Mahimahi (dolphin fish)	73	15.7	0.6	62	74	0.2	8
Mussels	81	12.2	1.9	48	243	0.7	22
Orange Roughy	107	12.5	6.0	17	54	0.1	52
Oysters (with shells)	59	6.0	2.1	47	95	0.5	34
Perch	76	16.2	0.8	75	51	0.2	10
Pompano	140	15.7	8.1	43	55	3.0	54
Red Snapper	85	17.5	1.1	31	37	0.2	13
Rockfish	80	15.9	1.3	29	51	0.3	16
Salmon	157	23.3	6.4	42	50	1.2	38
Scallops	75	14.3	0.6	28	137	0.1	8
Shark	111	17.8	3.8	43	67	0.8	33
Shrimp	66	14.0	0.7	131	149	0.2	10
Sole	69	14.2	0.9	40	62	0.2	12
Squid	78	13.2	1.2	198	37	0.3	14
Surimi	87	10.2	1.1	17	715	0.2	12
Swordfish	103	16.8	3.4	34	76	0.9	31
Trout	101	17.5	2.9	49	23	0.6	27
Tuna (canned)	116	22.7	2.1	36	333	0.6	17
Tuna (fresh)	92	19.9	0.8	38	32	0.2	8
Turbot	81	13.6	2.5	NA	127	0.7	29
Whitefish	114	16.2	5.0	51	43	0.8	41

PREFACE

Let's face it. Seafood eating is not only happy eating, it's healthful, too. Fish and shellfish are particularly healthful when prepared with an eye toward flavor and a focus on ingredients as well as cooking method. This attitude is what *Skinny Seafood* is all about—the ideal combination of good nutrition and gourmet satisfaction.

To achieve our goals, we first take advantage of wonderful fresh foods and the newer processed foods that are low in calories and fat. We use non-fat yogurt and mayonnaise and vegetable cooking sprays. We have lowered the amount of oil in most recipes, and use oils that are recognized to be more healthful. Herbs and spices round out the flavors. Using reduced amounts of margarine, butter, and oil, the results are still tasty and wholesome "skinny" recipes. As for cooking techniques, we have eliminated frying and capitalize on poaching, baking, package cooking, smoking, grilling, stir-frying, and microwave cooking.

By now, most Americans are well aware of the healthful qualities of cooked fish and shellfish, whether used as entrees, in salads, or in soups and stews. Nevertheless, many cooks are still hesitant about buying and preparing fish and shellfish. Probably the strongest reason for this hesitation is lack of confidence in purchasing and storing and in the cooking process itself.

It has been one of my consistent intentions during the writing of this book to make entering the realm of fish and shellfish a simpler and more comfortable experience. I grew up in the Boston area, and for many years my family was in the fish business. I began this book with strong and wonderful memories of cooking and eating fresh fish and shellfish. I am excited to share some favorite recipes from my youth and proud to have developed many new recipes that emphasize seafood's incredible richness and tastiness as well as its nutritional value and healthfulness.

During the research, development, and testing process, I have become a stronger advocate than ever before for the use of fish as an absolutely delicious meal focus. Fish contributes perfectly to America's ever-increasing health consciousness, and I am convinced that you will be delighted by the reactions of your family and guests when they experience these recipes. And when the cry goes up for "seconds," go for it without hesitation or guilt!

1.
FISH AND SHELLFISH: GOOD HEALTH, GOOD TASTE

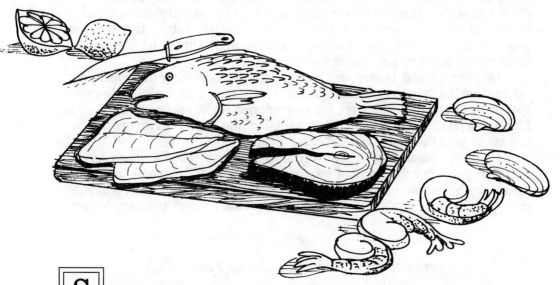

S even-eighths of the earth's surface is covered by water. That should tell us something. From those waters come the most healthful foods on the planet. Indeed, fish is the ideal choice to keep the heart healthy and the body in top shape.

Beef is beef; chicken is chicken; turkey is turkey—each a single species. But there are myriad fish and shellfish types and tastes. You can create months of delicious and nutritious fish and shellfish entrees without ever repeating a single dish. And eating even large portions of fish leaves diners without that "over-filled" feeling often experienced with other entrees.

Fish and most shellfish are low in saturated fat and in calories. Fish and shellfish are all rich in protein but vary widely in vitamin and mineral content. Most fish is rich in Vitamin B_{12}. Canned salmon is particularly high in many B vitamins. The best fish sources of calcium are

1

canned salmon and sardines, with their soft, edible bones. Oysters are the highest food source of zinc.

Lean fish, such as flounder, orange roughy, sole, halibut, catfish, red snapper, and perch, are particularly low in fat and saturated fat. Moderately fat fish include trout, pompano, and salmon. And even fish with the highest fat content, such as herring, bluefish, swordfish, and mackerel, are lower in fat than all but the leanest cuts of beef. When fish does have fat, it's largely the type of fat that's good for you.

Let's take an even closer look. Most fish have about 50 to 110 milligrams of cholesterol in a 4-ounce serving. That is as much or less than chicken or turkey. Caviar, shrimp, and lobster are the highest in cholesterol. The fish lowest in cholesterol are fresh halibut, orange roughy, tuna, and rockfish. In accordance with American Heart Association guidelines, eating fish is encouraged as a heart-healthy option.

As a bonus, fish contains omega-3 polyunsaturated fatty acids, fish oils that may reduce the risk of heart disease. Heart healthy diets include lots of fish. Omega-3 fatty acids also may be essential for optimal brain and eye development in infants. In general, the fattier the fish, the more omega-3s. Herring, whitefish, mackerel, and salmon, for example, have almost 2 grams per 4-ounce serving.

Of course, using butter and creamy sauces and frying fish increase both saturated fat content and calories. I have carefully designed the recipes in this book to avoid extra fat and calories while maintaining a high-taste profile. After all, it doesn't matter how healthful any recipe is if it isn't eaten because it doesn't taste good.

I am very pleased with the recipes in *Skinny Seafood* and am certain that you, your family, and your guests will be delighted as my taste-tester, my husband, has been. You may well find that the lakes, ponds, rivers, and seas of the world will replace dryland as your primary larder.

Purchasing and Storing Fresh and Frozen Fish

The surest way to obtain truly fresh fish is to find a reputable fish market that keeps close tabs on all its sources of fish and shellfish. Get to know the owner and staff, and trust them to steer you right. If possible, have your fish monger custom cut your fish, or purchase fresh whole fish that has been drawn and dressed. "Drawn" fish have had the entrails and usually the gills removed. "Dressed" fish have been drawn and have also had their scales removed. "Pan dressed" fish have had head, tail, and fins removed as well.

When purchasing fresh whole fish, look for bright, clear, full eyes. The flesh or skin should be shiny and brightly colored. Fresh fish will have pink or red gills as well as flesh that is firm and elastic enough to spring back when pressed with your finger. The aroma of fish should be fresh and mild. When purchasing fish fillets or steaks, look for a fresh aroma and a firm, moist texture.

Always avoid fish with cloudy, sunken eyes, gray or dark green gills, or a strong, very fishy odor. These signs are clear warnings that the fish is not fresh.

All fresh fish should be tightly wrapped in plastic and immediately refrigerated (32° F to 37° F) over a bed of ice. To enhance freshness, some cooks like to sprinkle fresh fish with salt or wine before storing it in the refrigerator. Use fresh fish within a day, if possible, and never use fresh fish more than two days after purchase.

Frozen Fish

If you purchase frozen fish, be absolutely certain that it is frozen solid. Ideally, frozen fish should be wrapped tightly in undamaged, moisture- and vapor-proof material. No odor should emanate from frozen fish. If you detect any aroma, notice any drying, deterioration, or spotting—or even suspect that the fish has been thawed and refrozen—run from it as fast as you can!

Frozen, uncooked fish will keep in a freezer three to six months. Fish with higher fat content do not store as long or as successfully as leaner fish. Store fish in your freezer at 0° F or colder.

Thaw fish in its wrapper in the refrigerator for 5 to 24 hours. Avoid thawing fish at room temperature. If necessary, fish can be quick-thawed by placing it, in its wrapping, in cold water. Allow approximately one hour per pound for thawing. Frozen fish can also be thawed in the micro-wave on 10 percent power for 10 to 15 seconds. Repeat if necessary until fish is nearly thawed. Then let the fish stand for another minute or two before cooking.

Never, under any circumstances, refreeze fish. Cooked leftover fish should be covered and stored in the refrigerator for use within two days.

Shellfish

If you are lucky enough to have access to a good fish market, purchase shellfish that is alive and fresh from the water. Live shellfish can be re-frigerated for a day or two. Place the live shellfish in a deep bowl or pan and cover with a damp paper towel or cloth. Use only *closed* clams or mussels for cooking.

Frozen shellfish is widely available year round throughout the na-tion. While frozen shellfish is certainly acceptable for use with the rec-ipes in this book, it will not provide the same degree of taste and texture as fresh shellfish.

Cooking Fish

For these recipes, I have recommended only healthful cooking methods and only small amounts, if any, of added fat. These methods include baking, poaching and steaming, broiling, and grilling.

Fish cooks quite quickly–particularly compared to beef, pork, and poultry–and must be watched closely. Overcooked fish is tough and virtually inedible. When fish is done, it is opaque rather than transparent or translucent. Translucent fish is undercooked. Cooked fish can also be tested for doneness by poking the tines of a fork into the thickest part of the fish. The flesh should flake easily. If the flesh resists flaking, the fish is underdone.

Cooking times are determined by the thickness of the fish and the cooking method. Check each recipe carefully, and pay close attention to the fish as it cooks. *Note:* When preparing clams and mussels, discard ones that remain closed after cooking.

2.
A BRIEF PRIMER ON CLEANING AND DRESSING FISH

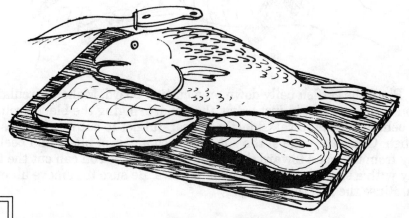

I f you purchase whole, uncleaned fish—or if you happen to have the good fortune to have a day's fresh catch—step one is cleaning. You also must gut and dress the fish unless you are going to fillet it, and usually even then it is a good idea to gut and dress.

Scaling Fish

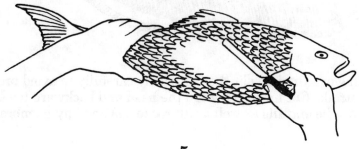

First, scale or skin the fish. To scale a fish, rinse it thoroughly. Grasp it by the tail, and using a dull knife (to avoid cutting into the flesh) or a fish scaler, scrape from the tail to the head in short, firm strokes. Rinse the stripped scales from the fish.

Skinning Catfish

Catfish do not have scales and must be skinned. While you can buy skinned catfish in most supermarkets and fish markets, you can, if necessary, remove the fish's incredibly tough skin at home. You will need your tool kit and a sharp knife. Although the method I advise doesn't sound very pleasant, it is effective.

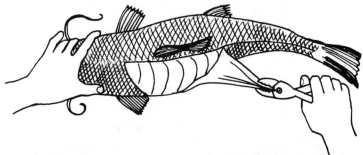

Place the catfish belly down on a cutting board. Make a circular incision through the skin just below the head, bringing the blade around and behind each pectoral (side) fin. Be careful not to cut into the flesh of the fish. Grasp the edge of the slit skin with a pair of pliers and peel it away from the head toward the tail in large strips. You can cut the fins away with a sharp knife or a pair of pincers. Be sure to remove all of the skin. Rinse the fish thoroughly.

Dressing

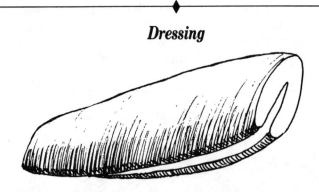

After scaling or skinning, slit the fish's belly carefully to avoid breaking into the entrails. Cut upward toward the head and backward toward the tail. Remove the entrails as well as all roe (eggs) and any membrane.

Cut the gills from beneath the gill cover. Cut off the head, fins, and tail, if desired. Rinse the fish thoroughly.

How to Cut Steaks from a Fish

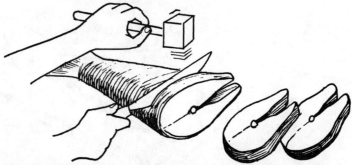

Flat fish, such as sole and flounder, are generally too thin to steak. To steak round fish, such as salmon and trout, use a sharp knife to slit at right angles down the backbone, marking off the steaks at desired thickness. Place the knife in each slit and use a mallet or rolling pin to tap the knife through the backbone. Rinse the steaks thoroughly. *Note:* Each steak will have a piece of backbone in its center.

How to Fillet Round and Flat Fish

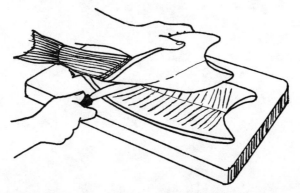

Round fish, such as bass and trout, and flat fish, such as sole and flounder, can be filleted by making shallow cuts crosswise behind the gills and at the tail end. These cuts should be deep enough to reach just to the backbone. Insert a sharp knife and slide it horizontally from the head to the tail of the fish. Follow the backbone closely with your blade. A clean lengthwise cut should produce a boneless fillet.

Place the fillet on a cutting board with the skin side down. To separate skin and flesh, use a very sharp knife and hold the blade nearly horizontal to the board. Work the blade from the narrow end of the fillet to the wide end to separate skin and flesh. Keep the skin very taut as you move the blade. The result should be a clean fillet from each side of the fish. Remove any small bones with a small knife or your fingers. Rinse the fillets thoroughly.

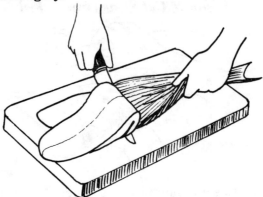

3.
THIN FISH

Trout
♦
Sole
♦
Tilapia
♦
Perch
♦
Flounder
♦
Whitefish

STEAMED LAKE TROUT WITH TOMATO-GINGER SAUCE

Steaming fish is similar to poaching except for the important difference that the fish always stays above the level of the cooking liquid. Use a steamer, or improvise by using an inverted bowl in a covered pan. Add water half-way up the side of the bowl; do not cover the bowl. Place the fish in a single layer on a plate or greased rack that will fit comfortably inside the cooking pan. Center the plate on the inverted bowl. Heat the water to boiling, reduce to simmer, then cover the pan and steam the fish. Some of the fish that we steam with great success are trout, bluefish, cod, flounder, salmon, and scrod.

4 Servings

- 2 whole lake trout, about 10 to 12 ozs. each; dress and discard head and tail; you may wish to have the fishmonger bone the fish
- 2 teaspoons light soy sauce
- 2 tablespoons orange rind, grated
- ½ cup pickled ginger (recipe follows)
- ½ teaspoon sesame seeds
- 2 cups cucumber, seeded, thinly sliced
- 1 cup tomato, peeled, seeded, chopped

S team trout, sprinkled with soy sauce and orange rind, about 5 minutes or until done. The fish will be opaque and slightly firm to the touch. Cool 5 minutes. Cut each fish in half, and set each piece of trout on an individual plate.

In a bowl, toss ginger with sesame seeds, cucumber, and tomatoes. Spoon mixture onto center of each piece of fish. Serve hot. This is especially good with hot Japanese buckwheat noodles.

Nutritional Data

PER SERVING		EXCHANGES	
Calories:	249	Milk:	0.0
Fat (gm):	5.3	Veg.:	1.0
Sat. fat (gm):	1.0	Fruit:	1.0
Cholesterol (mg):	81	Bread:	0.0
Sodium (mg):	155	Meat:	3.0
% Calories from fat:	19	Fat:	0.0

PICKLED GINGER

Pickled ginger can be purchased at gourmet food shops and from some Japanese restaurants. It has a good, spicy, palate-cleansing aftertaste. It is fun and interesting to make your own Pickled Ginger.

---

5 Servings
(about 1¼ cups)

½ lb. ginger, peeled, sliced very thin
1½ cups boiling water
1 cup rice vinegar
2 cups sugar
¼ teaspoon salt

When peeling ginger, discard small knobs. Use a potato peeler for easy peeling. To slice, use a food processor fitted with a fine-slicing blade, or cut the ginger in very thin slices, using a small, sharp knife. Put ginger in bowl and cover with boiling water. Let ginger stand 1 minute, then drain well.

In a small, separate, non-metallic bowl, mix together vinegar, sugar, and salt. Stir sauce into the well-drained ginger. Cover bowl with plastic wrap and let stand at room temperature 45 minutes. Still covered with plastic wrap, refrigerate overnight or up to 24 hours before serving. Drain ginger well before serving.

To store, leave ginger in liquid in covered container and refrigerate until needed. Drain well before serving.

Nutritional Data

PER SERVING		EXCHANGES	
Calories:	127	Milk:	0.0
Fat (gm):	0.3	Veg.:	1.0
Sat. fat (gm):	0.1	Fruit:	1.5
Cholesterol (mg):	0	Bread:	1.0
Sodium (mg):	42	Meat:	1.0
% Calories from fat:	2	Fat:	1.0

PAN-FRIED TROUT

Rainbow trout are small speckled trout about 8 to 10 inches long. This lake fish is usually served with its tail and head intact although not in this recipe. My fishmonger even bones them for easy eating.

4 Servings

2 small, whole rainbow trout, about 10 ozs. each; ask fishmonger to bone trout and discard head and tail

⅓ cup white cornmeal

¼ teaspoon each; freshly ground black pepper; anise seeds

½ cup cilantro or parsley, minced

Canola oil, or non-stick cooking spray

Run fingers over fish to check if there are any remaining bones. If so, remove them with kitchen tweezers. Cut fish in half. Wash fish and pat dry.

Mix together cornmeal, spices, and cilantro. Roll fish in mixture, pressing it gently into fish.

Fry fish in sprayed non-stick frying pan over medium heat until cooked. Turn once. Fish will be browned and crisp on outside, firm to the touch, and flake easily when prodded with fork. Cut each fish in half vertically for 4 servings.

Using a spatula transfer the trout to individual plates. Serve hot.

Nutritional Data

PER SERVING		EXCHANGES	
Calories:	208	Milk:	0.0
Fat (gm):	5.2	Veg.:	0.0
Sat. fat (gm):	1.0	Fruit:	0.0
Cholesterol (mg):	81	Bread:	0.5
Sodium (mg):	45	Meat:	3.0
% Calories from fat:	23	Fat:	0.0

TROUT WITH MANGO AND BLUEBERRY SAUCE

6 Servings

Mango-Blueberry Sauce
- 3   medium-large ripe mangoes, peeled
- 1   cup blueberries, picked over, washed, drained
- 2   tablespoons sugar
- 3   tablespoons raspberry vinegar

Trout
-     Olive oil, or non-stick cooking spray
- ½   cup red onion, chopped
- 1¼–1½ lbs. trout, filleted
- 3   tablespoons lime juice, freshly squeezed
- 2   tablespoons capers

Mango-Blueberry Sauce: Remove pulp from mangoes. Heat sugar in non-stick saucepan until it begins to caramelize. Stir in vinegar and fruit. Stir and cook over medium heat 3 minutes. Reserve and reheat before serving.

Trout: Spray a non-stick frying pan with oil. Saute onions over medium heat until tender, stirring occasionally. Pan fry trout until cooked, turning once. Fish will turn opaque and flake easily when prodded with fork. Remove to serving dish. Sprinkle with lime juice and capers.

Spoon Mango-Blueberry Sauce around the fish fillets. Serve hot.

Nutritional Data

PER SERVING		EXCHANGES	
Calories:	216	Milk:	0.0
Fat (gm):	3.6	Veg.:	0.0
Sat. fat (gm):	0.7	Fruit:	1.5
Cholesterol (mg):	54	Bread:	0.0
Sodium (mg):	29	Meat:	2.5
% Calories from fat:	14	Fat:	0.0

Trout Pâté Pita Pizzas

The cooked trout is mashed with flavorful herbs to make a tasty fish Pâté. This is spread over the pita pizzas, heated, and served.

---

6 Servings

- 3 whole-wheat pita breads
  Olive oil, or non-stick cooking spray
- 1 lb. trout fillets
- 3 cloves garlic, minced
- ½ cup white mushrooms, chopped
- ¼ cup parsley, minced
- ½ teaspoon each: thyme; sage
- 1 tomato, sliced thin

Split pita breads in half. Set aside.

Spray or oil a non-stick frying pan. Sprinkle trout with garlic and mushrooms and saute on both sides until done. Fish is cooked when it flakes easily and is just firm to the touch. Cool fish. Puree fish, garlic, and mushrooms. Flavor with parsley, thyme, and sage.

Spread trout pâté over pita bread halves, and center a tomato slice on each piece. Using a spatula, put pita pizzas on cookie sheet.

Preheat oven to 425° F., and bake 7 to 10 minutes or until breads are just crisp. Remove to serving plate and serve hot. Accompany with a crisp salad.

Nutritional Data

PER SERVING		EXCHANGES	
Calories:	149	Milk:	0.0
Fat (gm):	3.0	Veg.:	0.0
Sat. fat (gm):	0.5	Fruit:	0.0
Cholesterol (mg):	43	Bread:	0.5
Sodium (mg):	131	Meat:	2.0
% Calories from fat:	18	Fat:	0.0

SOLE WITH ROSEMARY POTATOES

Rosemary adds a pungent flavor to baked potatoes.

6 Servings

```
    4  baking potatoes
       Canola oil, or non-stick cooking spray
    2  tablespoons rosemary
   ½  teaspoon garlic powder
   ¼  teaspoon pepper
1¼–1½  lbs. sole fillets
    4  shallots, minced
    1  small red onion, chopped
    1  large clove garlic, minced
```

Preheat oven to 400° F. Scrub potatoes and cut each into 6 or 8 wedges. Set wedges on sprayed, non-stick cookie sheet. Sprinkle potatoes with rosemary, garlic powder, and pepper.

Bake potatoes about 45 minutes or until they are golden brown, crisp, and done to taste. Turn potatoes 3 to 4 times while baking.

About 15 minutes before potatoes are done, wash fish and pat dry. Saute shallots, onion, and garlic in sprayed non-stick frying pan until soft, stirring occasionally over medium heat. Fold each fillet of fish in half and place in pan with shallots, onion, and garlic. Cook fish over medium-high heat 2 to 4 minutes. Turn fish once, carefully with spatula, picking up pieces of shallots and garlic as you do so. Continue cooking only a few minutes, until done to taste. The fish will be opaque and flake easily when prodded with fork.

Serve fish with garlic, onion, and shallots over and around it and hot rosemary potatoes on the side.

Nutritional Data

PER SERVING		EXCHANGES	
Calories:	186	Milk:	0.0
Fat (gm):	1.1	Veg.:	0.0
Sat. fat (gm):	0.3	Fruit:	0.0
Cholesterol (mg):	44	Bread:	1.0
Sodium (mg):	75	Meat:	2.0
% Calories from fat:	6	Fat:	0.0

SOLE WITH FENNEL

You might want to make a cornbread muffin in a scallop shell as an accompaniment.

4 Servings

- 2 fennel bulbs, cut in half, reserve stalks
  Canola oil, or non-stick cooking spray
- 1 cup onion, chopped
- 1 teaspoon tarragon vinegar
- ¼ teaspoon each: salt; pepper
- 4 large sea scallops
- 1¼ lbs. sole, cut into 4 fillets
- ½ cup flat-leaf parsley, chopped

Core fennel bulbs and slice thin. Chop reserved fennel stalks.
Cook fennel and stalks in 2 cups lightly salted water over high
heat 3 minutes or until just tender. Strain. Divide and arrange on 4
warm plates.

Saute onion in sprayed non-stick frying pan. Stir in vinegar, salt,
and pepper. Add scallops and fry 3 minutes on each side or until opaque
and just firm to the touch.

At the same time, cook sole, turning once carefully, until done.
Watch fish closely, as it cooks quickly. Fish is done when it is opaque
and flakes easily.

Using a spatula, place sole on plates over the fennel. Place one sea
scallop on each plate next to the sole. Sprinkle with parsley and serve
hot.

Nutritional Data

PER SERVING		EXCHANGES	
Calories:	207	Milk:	0.0
Fat (gm):	2.3	Veg.:	0.0
Sat. fat (gm):	0.4	Fruit:	0.0
Cholesterol (mg):	94	Bread:	0.0
Sodium (mg):	377	Meat:	4.0
% Calories from fat:	10	Fat:	0.0

SOLE AND SHRIMP WITH TEQUILA

Of all the fish we eat and enjoy, sole is perhaps the most delicate and light tasting. It goes well with a great variety of seafoods, herbs, spices, and sauces. The name Dover sole comes from the Atlantic variety, which was sold at the Dover, England, port. The less glamorous flounder has been renamed gray sole or white sole, probably because it is also a flat fish.

4 Servings

- 1¼ lbs. sole, cut into 4 fillets
- ⅛ teaspoon salt
- ¼ teaspoon white pepper
- 8 jumbo shrimp, peeled, deveined, butterflied
  Canola oil, or non-stick cooking spray
- 4 large shallots, minced
- 1 lb. spinach, washed, dried, trimmed
- 2 tablespoons honey mustard
- ¼ cup tequila
- 1 lime, sliced thin

P reheat oven to 325–350° F. Wash sole and pat dry. Season lightly with salt and pepper. Spray a shallow baking pan and set fish, folded in half, on pan. Set aside.

To butterfly shrimp, make a cut along the back, opening the shrimp but not cutting all the way through. Set aside.

Spray a non-stick frying pan. Saute shallots until tender, stirring occasionally, about 5 minutes. Add spinach, sweating it, covered, and stirring occasionally until soft, about 5 minutes. Spoon spinach-shallot mixture into folds of the sole. Add shrimp to pan. Mix mustard with tequila and sprinkle over all.

Bake fish and shrimp 15 minutes or until cooked. Fish will turn opaque and be just firm to the touch. Shrimp will turn a pinkish-white color. Using a spatula, put fish on individual serving dishes and top with shrimp and lime slices. Serve hot. Good with rice or pilaf.

Nutritional Data

PER SERVING		EXCHANGES	
Calories:	217	Milk:	0.0
Fat (gm):	2.1	Veg.:	1.0
Sat. fat (gm):	0.5	Fruit:	0.0
Cholesterol (mg):	110	Bread:	0.0
Sodium (mg):	510	Meat:	3.5
% Calories from fat:	9	Fat:	0.0

MICROWAVE SOLE WITH CUCUMBER SAUCE

Sole is one of the most popular fish sold. Any flat fish can be substituted, such as flounder, gray sole, or lemon sole. The best sole is caught off the coast of England.

4 Servings

Cucumber Sauce
- 1 cup cucumber, peeled, seeded, chopped
- 1 cup non-fat ricotta cheese
- ¼ cup non-fat plain yogurt
- 2 tablespoons dill weed, chopped
- ½ teaspoon rosemary
- 3 cloves garlic, minced

Sole
- Olive oil, or non-stick cooking spray
- ½ cup onion, minced
- 1¼ lbs. Dover sole fillets, 4 portions
- 1 cucumber, scored with fork, cut in thin slices

Cucumber Sauce: Using a food processor fitted with steel blade, mix together cucumber, ricotta cheese, yogurt, dill weed, rosemary, and garlic. Spoon sauce into glass bowl, cover, and refrigerate until serving.

Sole: Use a microwave-safe glass dish or glass pie plate, sprayed and sprinkled with onions. Arrange fish tucked under so that it is even in thickness, and place it evenly on plate. Cover securely with plastic wrap for the microwave. Put plate in microwave and cook 2 minutes on High. If fish is not cooked, continue until done. Fish is done when it is opaque and flakes easily when prodded with fork.

Remove from microwave and place sole on individual plates. Arrange cucumbers in overlapping pattern on fish to resemble scales.

Spoon Cucumber Sauce on the side. Serve hot.

Nutritional Data

PER SERVING		EXCHANGES	
Calories:	167	Milk:	0.0
Fat (gm):	2.7	Veg.:	1.0
Sat. fat (gm):	0.4	Fruit:	0.0
Cholesterol (mg):	72	Bread:	0.0
Sodium (mg):	137	Meat:	3.0
% Calories from fat:	15	Fat:	0.0

PAN-FRIED TILAPIA WITH APPLE SLICES

Fruit is a good accompaniment to most fish. Here, we slice the apples and cook the fish on them. This transfers a delicate flavor to the fish. This dish is good served with hot sauerkraut.

4 Servings

  2 large cooking apples, such as Granny Smith or Golden Delicious, peeled, cored, sliced in rounds or slices
      Non-stick cooking spray
  ½ teaspoon ground cinnamon
  1 teaspoon sugar
  ¼ teaspoon each: dried thyme; white pepper
1¼–1½ lbs. tilapia fillets
  2 tablespoons dry white wine

S lice apples in thin rounds or slices. Spray a non-stick frying pan. Mix cinnamon with sugar and sprinkle on bottom of pan. Add apples and cook over medium heat until just soft; turn over.

Sprinkle thyme and pepper over tilapia fillets. Sprinkle with wine. Cook in same pan until done, turning once. Fish will turn opaque and will flake easily when prodded with fork. Using a spatula, remove fish and apples to individual dishes. Serve hot.

Nutritional Data

PER SERVING		EXCHANGES	
Calories:	199	Milk:	0.0
Fat (gm):	3.1	Veg.:	0.0
Sat. fat (gm):	0.0	Fruit:	0.5
Cholesterol (mg):	128	Bread:	0.0
Sodium (mg):	54	Meat:	3.0
% Calories from fat:	15	Fat:	0.0

PERCH WITH PICKLED RED ONION RINGS

In the Midwest fresh-water perch is plentiful, but it is also available frozen. It is a small fish, found in the lakes and rivers of the Midwest and Canada. When using frozen fish, always make sure that it is not dried out and that there are no ice crystals inside the package.

4 Servings

Pickled Red Onion Rings

- 1½ cups red onions, thinly sliced
- ⅓ cup sugar
- ⅓ cup red wine, or cider vinegar
- ¼ teaspoon each: salt; anise seeds

Perch

- 1 teaspoon each: thyme; marjoram; chopped parsley
- 1 lb. perch fillets (if frozen, defrost in refrigerator)

Pickled Red Onion Rings: Separate onions into rings and put them in ceramic bowl. Mix together remaining ingredients and toss with onion rings. Cover and refrigerate overnight. Toss once or twice while onions are marinating. Taste to adjust seasonings before serving. To serve, drain onions and spoon them onto plate with fish.

Perch: Place fish on microwave-proof dish and sprinkle with thyme, marjoram, and parsley. Cover with waxed paper. Microwave on High 5 minutes. Rotate plate once during cooking. Remove fish from microwave and check to see if it is cooked. Fish will be opaque in color and flake easily when prodded with fork. If it does not seem cooked, microwave another minute or until done to taste; do not overcook.

Remove plate from microwave and, using slotted spoon, divide fish onto dishes. Serve with Pickled Red Onion Rings.

Nutritional Data

PER SERVING		EXCHANGES	
Calories:	144	Milk:	0.0
Fat (gm):	1.1	Veg.:	1.0
Sat. fat (gm):	0.2	Fruit:	0.0
Cholesterol (mg):	100	Bread:	0.0
Sodium (mg):	115	Meat:	2.0
% Calories from fat:	7	Fat:	0.0

PERCH OR BUTTERFISH WITH PINEAPPLE-GINGER SAUCE

Butterfish is an Atlantic fish, flavorful, tender, and small. It is interesting to me how the recipes have changed through the years. Originally when preparing a stir-fry recipe, you would start with from 4 to 6 tablespoons of oil; now we can cook the same recipe with just a spray of low-fat vegetable oil.

6 Servings

Marinade
- 2 tablespoons light soy sauce
- 2 tablespoons dry white wine
- 2 cloves garlic, minced

Fish
- 1¼ lbs. perch, or butterfish, fillets, cut into serving-size pieces
- Canola oil, or non-stick cooking spray
- 3 egg whites, slightly beaten
- 1 tablespoon cornstarch

Pineapple-Ginger Sauce
- 1 cup bean sprouts, blanched in hot water, drained
- ½ teaspoon ginger root, freshly grated
- 1 can (8 ozs.) pineapple chunks, no sugar added
- ¼ cup pineapple juice

Marinade: Combine soy sauce, wine, and garlic. Put fish in shallow glass dish and sprinkle with marinade. Let fish stand 30 minutes. Drain.

Fish: Spray a non-stick frying pan with oil. Dip fish in beaten egg whites mixed with cornstarch. (Reserve remaining dip.) Saute fish until cooked on both sides. Fish will turn opaque when cooked.

Pineapple-Ginger Sauce: In a saucepan, heat remaining egg whites with ginger and bean sprouts. Add pineapple chunks and juice.

Put cooked fish on serving platter and drizzle Pineapple-Ginger Sauce over fish. Serve hot. Good with whole-wheat noodles or cooked rice.

Nutritional Data

PER SERVING		EXCHANGES	
Calories:	130	Milk:	0.0
Fat (gm):	0.9	Veg.:	0.0
Sat. fat (gm):	0.2	Fruit:	0.5
Cholesterol (mg):	83	Bread:	0.0
Sodium (mg):	272	Meat:	2.0
% Calories from fat:	6	Fat:	0.0

Microwave Perch with Honeydew Salsa

Why not use fruit in a salsa; it is tasty, refreshing, and pretty to see.

---

4 Servings

Honeydew Salsa

- 2 cups honeydew, diced
- 1 green bell pepper, seeded, chopped
- 3 green onions, minced
- ¼ cup cilantro, minced
- 2 tablespoons raspberry vinegar
- ⅛ teaspoon red pepper flakes, optional

Perch

- 1¼–1½ lbs. perch fillets, defrosted or fresh
- 3 tablespoons raspberry vinegar
- ½ cup raspberries, defrosted or fresh

Honeydew Salsa: Toss all salsa ingredients in a small glass bowl. Cover lightly and refrigerate until serving time. Toss salsa again before serving and taste to adjust seasonings.

Perch: Use a glass pie plate or other microwave-safe dish. Arrange fish in dish, and sprinkle with vinegar and raspberries. Cover dish securely with plastic wrap for the microwave. Cook in microwave 3 to 4 minutes on High. If fish is not cooked, continue cooking until done to taste. Fish is done when it is opaque and flakes easily when prodded with fork.

Remove plate from microwave and discard plastic wrap. (Remove wrap away from you to avoid escaping steam, or cut slits in wrap with small, sharp knife before removing.) Place fish on each plate, and spoon Honeydew Salsa alongside. Serve hot.

Nutritional Data

PER SERVING		EXCHANGES	
Calories:	173	Milk:	0.0
Fat (gm):	1.5	Veg.:	0.0
Sat. fat (gm):	0.3	Fruit:	0.5
Cholesterol (mg):	125	Bread:	0.0
Sodium (mg):	96	Meat:	3.0
% Calories from fat:	8	Fat:	0.0

MICROWAVE FLOUNDER WITH MINT DRESSING

For best results, have fillets at even thickness. If the fillet tapers off and one side is thicker, tuck the thinner end under so that the fillets are uniform.

4 Servings

Mint Dressing

½ cup non-fat plain yogurt
¼ cup non-fat ricotta cheese
2 teaspoons stone-ground mustard
3 tablespoons fresh mint leaves, minced

Flounder

1¼ lbs. flounder fillets, 4 serving pieces
2 tablespoons fresh mint leaves, minced

Mint Dressing: Mix together yogurt, ricotta cheese, mustard, and mint leaves in a small glass bowl. Cover and refrigerate until ready to serve. Mix before serving, and taste to adjust seasonings.

Flounder: Using a microwave-safe glass dish, arrange fish evenly. Sprinkle fish with mint leaves. Cover dish securely with plastic wrap for the microwave. Place in microwave and cook 2 to 4 minutes on High. If fish is not cooked, continue cooking until fish is opaque and flakes easily when prodded with fork.

Remove from microwave and cut slits in plastic wrap to expel steam before discarding. Spoon Mint Dressing onto individual dishes and set fish over it.

Nutritional Data

PER SERVING		EXCHANGES	
Calories:	150	Milk:	0.0
Fat (gm):	2.0	Veg.:	0.0
Sat. fat (gm):	0.4	Fruit:	0.0
Cholesterol (mg):	77	Bread:	0.0
Sodium (mg):	142	Meat:	3.0
% Calories from fat:	12	Fat:	0.0

FLOUNDER SANDWICH WITH HORSERADISH SAUCE

Use a mild bottled horseradish for the sauce. This hot and pungent flavoring makes a wonderful, spicy sauce that is delicious in the sandwich.

4 Servings

Beer Marinade
- 1 teaspoon olive oil
- ½ cup onions, chopped
- ½ cup light beer
- 3 tablespoons cider vinegar
- ½ teaspoon dry mustard
- ¼ teaspoon each: ground cumin; pepper

Flounder
1¼–1½ lbs. flounder fillets

Horseradish Sauce
- 1½ cups non-fat plain yogurt
- 1–2 tablespoons prepared white horseradish

Accompaniments
- Olive oil, or non-stick cooking spray
- 4 slices oatmeal bread
- 4 lettuce leaves
- 4 thin slices tomato
- 4 thin slices onion

Beer Marinade: Combine all ingredients and pour into self-sealing plastic bag. Add flounder pieces and seal bag securely. Turn bag several times so that all surfaces of fish are touched by marinade. Set bag in shallow dish and refrigerate 1 to 2 hours, turning bag once or twice. Remove flounder from marinade; discard marinade.

Flounder: Spray a skillet with oil, and fry flounder fillets until done, turning once. Fish is done when it is opaque and flakes easily when prodded with fork.

Horseradish Sauce: In a small bowl, stir horseradish into yogurt.

Accompaniments: Toast bread and place on individual plates. Brush bread with Horseradish Sauce. Place a lettuce leaf on bread, with fish on top. Place tomato and onion slices on the flounder. Pass extra Horseradish Sauce at the table and serve with sliced pickles.

Nutritional Data

PER SERVING		EXCHANGES	
Calories:	282	Milk:	0.0
Fat (gm):	3.2	Veg.:	0.5
Sat. fat (gm):	0.5	Fruit:	0.0
Cholesterol (mg):	77	Bread:	1.0
Sodium (mg):	425	Meat:	3.0
% Calories from fat:	10	Fat:	0.0

BAKED WHITEFISH
WITH SUN-DRIED TOMATO STUFFING

Stuffing possibilities are almost endless. Any successful combination of vegetables and crumbs make this possible. With tomatoes and just a taste of slivered almonds, this recipe takes on a Spanish air. The whole fish makes a beautiful presentation for family or company, but this recipe can also be prepared as fillets.

8 Servings

Sun-Dried Tomato Stuffing

Olive oil, or non-stick cooking spray
- 1 cup onions, chopped
- ¼ cup shallots, minced
- 1 cup celery, sliced
- ¾ cup sun-dried tomatoes, reconstituted in hot water, shredded
- 2 cups tomatoes, chopped
- ½ cup dry breadcrumbs
- ¼ teaspoon each: chervil; white pepper

Fish

- 2 lbs. whitefish, red snapper, or sea bass, whole, with trimmed off belly flap, or filleted
- 2 tablespoons sliced almonds

Sun-Dried Tomato Stuffing: Spray non-stick frying pan and saute onions, shallots, and celery over medium heat until tender, stirring occasionally. Add sun-dried and chopped tomatoes and continue cooking 5 minutes. Mix in breadcrumbs, chervil, and white pepper. Mix all ingredients together.

Fish: Place fish in sprayed baking dish, and spoon stuffing over it. Sprinkle with almonds.

Preheat oven to 375° F. and bake fish and stuffing 15–20 minutes or until fish is cooked. Fish will turn opaque and be firm to the touch. Remove from oven and serve hot.

Nutritional Data

PER SERVING		EXCHANGES	
Calories:	140	Milk:	0.0
Fat (gm):	4.8	Veg.:	2.0
Sat. fat (gm):	0.2	Fruit:	0.0
Cholesterol (mg):	34	Bread:	0.0
Sodium (mg):	107	Meat:	2.0
% Calories from fat:	30	Fat:	0.0

DOOR COUNTY FISH BOIL

A fish boil is a regional tradition from Wisconsin, usually prepared outdoors with great flair. A huge kettle is used, and at the end of the cooking, it usually overflows in a great flurry. Here we have adapted this midwestern dish for the indoor kitchen, with no overflowing, please.

6 Servings

½ teaspoon salt
6 small red potatoes, scrubbed
6 small onions, peeled
1 lb. whitefish fillets, cut into 4–6 pieces
Lemon wedges
Parsley for garnish

Fill stockpot half full of water and bring to a boil. Stir in salt. Cook potatoes and onions about 15 minutes or until tender. Place fish in strainer and lower it into water. Cook 6 to 7 minutes or until fish is opaque and flakes easily. Do not overcook.

Transfer fish to platter, and surround it with potatoes and onions, lemon wedges, and parsley. Bring to table hot. Round out this Wisconsin dish with corn, coleslaw, and a cherry dessert.

Nutritional Data

PER SERVING		EXCHANGES	
Calories:	155	Milk:	0.0
Fat (gm):	3.7	Veg.:	0.5
Sat. fat (gm):	0.6	Fruit:	0.0
Cholesterol (mg):	36	Bread:	1.0
Sodium (mg):	212	Meat:	1.5
% Calories from fat:	21	Fat:	0.0

4.
MEDIUM-THICK FISH

Red Snapper
Cod
Scrod
Bass
Mahimahi
Catfish
Orange Roughy
Rockfish

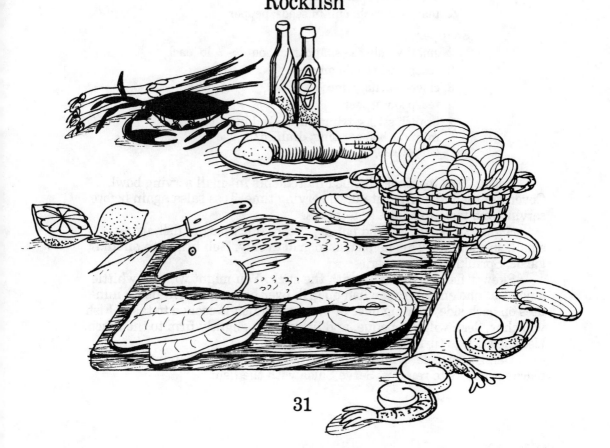

SALSA RED SNAPPER GRILLED ON A STICK

What a surprise to find this interesting method of grilling small whole red snapper on sleepy Mesmeola Beach in Mexico! Rustic barbecues were set up on the beach, and the snappers had a trimmed branch horizontally skewered through them. The fish were rubbed with oil and spices and served with lots of fresh lime and cold Mexican beer. To reproduce this cooking technique in your own yard, hunt for appropriate-size branches and trim them. If branches are not available, use a sturdy chopstick or, if all else fails, set the snappers on a bed of parsley or dill and grill them according to the recipe below.

2 Servings

Salsa

  2 cups tomatoes, peeled, seeded, and chopped
  ½ teaspoon jalapeño pepper, seeded (wear rubber gloves when handling)
  3 teaspoons lime juice, freshly squeezed
  1¼ cup cilantro, chopped
  ¼ teaspoon each: cumin seeds; pepper

Snapper

  2 small whole red snappers, about ½–¾ lb. each
  2 teaspoons canola oil
  3 cloves garlic, minced
  ¼ teaspoon pepper
  2 branch sticks, trimmed, soaked in water 20 minutes before using, drained (or use chopsticks)

Salsa: Toss together all salsa ingredients in small serving bowl. Cover lightly and refrigerate until serving time. Toss salsa again before serving and taste to adjust seasonings.

Snapper: Wash fish and pat dry. Score thick part of fish, using small, sharp knife. This helps fish to grill evenly. Rub fish with oil and garlic. Sprinkle with pepper.

Skewer fish horizontally with the stick. You might want to whittle a point at one end. Arrange fish on grill over hot coals. Grill fish 5 minutes on each side, turning once or twice until fish is cooked to taste. Fish will char, flesh will be opaque, and fish will be slightly firm to the touch. Use the stick to turn fish.

Using a spatula, transfer fish to individual plates, leaving sticks in place for guests to remove. Serve Salsa with the fish.

Nutritional Data

PER SERVING		EXCHANGES	
Calories:	345	Milk:	0.0
Fat (gm):	8.7	Veg.:	2.0
Sat. fat (gm):	1.1	Fruit:	0.0
Cholesterol (mg):	83	Bread:	0.0
Sodium (mg):	139	Meat:	4.5
% Calories from fat:	22	Fat:	1.0

RED SNAPPER KABOBS WITH YELLOW PEPPER SAUCE

Kabobs make a very easy and festive presentation. You can be creative by substituting vegetables of your choice that go with the sauce. We use yellow bell peppers for the sauce, but you can substitute red or green bell peppers. Red snapper is a medium-firm fish from the warm Caribbean waters, and it is mild tasting. You can substitute black sea bass or mahimahi.

4 Servings

Yellow Pepper Sauce

- 3 yellow bell peppers, seeded, chopped
- 1 large yellow tomato, skinned, seeded, chopped
- 1 teaspoon each: freshly squeezed lemon juice; lemon rind
- 3 cloves garlic, peeled
- 2 well-drained anchovies
- ¼ teaspoon each: oregano; white pepper
- 2 tablespoons non-fat plain yogurt

Snapper Kabobs

- 4 double-pronged skewers
- 1¼ lbs. red snapper fillets
- 16 pods of snow peas, trimmed
- 16 cherry tomatoes, washed, drained

Yellow Pepper Sauce: In a food processor fitted with steel blade, puree peppers and tomato with lemon juice, lemon rind, garlic, anchovies, oregano, white pepper, and yogurt. Spoon sauce into a bowl. Cover and refrigerate until ready to serve.

Snapper Kabobs: Cut fish into 2-inch pieces. Thread fish pieces onto skewers with snow peas and cherry tomatoes. Preheat broiler. Set kabobs on broiler rack, about 6 inches from heat, broil 3 minutes, turn, and broil another 3 minutes; then cook until done to taste, rotating kabobs every 3 minutes. Remember not to overcook fish. Fish is done when it turns opaque and flakes easily when prodded with fork.

Place a kabob on each plate and serve hot with Yellow Pepper Sauce.

Nutritional Data

PER SERVING		EXCHANGES	
Calories:	199	Milk:	0.0
Fat (gm):	2.6	Veg.:	1.5
Sat. fat (gm):	0.5	Fruit:	0.0
Cholesterol (mg):	54	Bread:	0.0
Sodium (mg):	152	Meat:	3.0
% Calories from fat:	12	Fat:	0.0

COD WITH RED ONION SAUCE

Cod was so important to the early Massachusetts settlers that there is now a cod hanging in the statehouse in Boston. It is a large fish, average weight about 10 pounds, and it is caught mainly off Newfoundland and New England. Scrod is young cod. Cod is sold smoked, salted, filleted, frozen, steaked, and as whole fish.

4 Servings

Red Onion Sauce

- ¼ cup vegetable or chicken stock
- 3 cups red onions, thinly sliced
- ½ cup currants, or dark raisins
- 1 cup dry white wine
- ½ teaspoon thyme
  Black pepper, freshly ground

Cod

  Olive oil, or non-stick cooking spray
- 1¼–1½ lbs. cod fillets, cut into 4 pieces
- ¼ teaspoon each: salt; pepper

Red Onion Sauce: Heat stock in saucepan over medium heat. Stir in red onions. Cook, partially covered, stirring often until onions are soft. Stir in currants, white wine, thyme, and freshly ground black pepper to taste.

Continue cooking uncovered until most liquid has evaporated. Taste to adjust seasonings. Good served hot, warm, or cold. Set aside until serving time.

Cod: Spray broiler pan. Wash and pat dry fish. Sprinkle cod with salt and pepper. Place fish on broiler pan, and cook about 6-inches from heat source for about 5 minutes. Turn once if necessary. Fish is done when it turns opaque, is just firm to the touch, and will flake easily when prodded.

Using a spatula, transfer fish to individual plates and top with a dollop of Red Onion Sauce. Serve hot.

Nutritional Data

PER SERVING		EXCHANGES	
Calories:	204	Milk:	0.0
Fat (gm):	1.2	Veg.:	1.5
Sat. fat (gm):	0.2	Fruit:	0.0
Cholesterol (mg):	56	Bread:	0.0
Sodium (mg):	268	Meat:	3.0
% Calories from fat:	5	Fat:	0.0

COD STEAKS BAKED WITH PLUM TOMATOES

The rule of thumb is that you bake fish 10 minutes per inch of thickness. But I always recommend that fish be cooked to taste, and that if you are doubtful, lean toward undercooking.

4 Servings

Olive oil, or non-stick cooking spray
1¼–1½ lbs. cod steaks (4 steaks)
1 can (16 ozs.) plum tomatoes, crushed, juice included
½ teaspoon each: garlic powder; oregano; basil
1 cup onions, chopped

S pray a 10-inch pie plate. Wash and pat cod dry. Place fish in plate. Spread tomatoes over fish and sprinkle with garlic powder, oregano, basil, and onions.

Preheat oven to 375° F. Bake fish about 10 to 15 minutes or until cooked. Fish is done when it turns opaque, is slightly firm to the touch, and will flake easily when prodded.

To serve, use a large spoon or spatula to transfer fish to individual plates. Surround fish with vegetables. Serve hot with Italian bread sticks.

Nutritional Data

PER SERVING		EXCHANGES	
Calories:	145	Milk:	0.0
Fat (gm):	1.2	Veg.:	1.5
Sat. fat (gm):	0.2	Fruit:	0.0
Cholesterol (mg):	56	Bread:	0.0
Sodium (mg):	266	Meat:	3.0
% Calories from fat:	8	Fat:	0.0

SKINNY SEAFOOD

38

Scrod with Chili Oyster Sauce

Oyster sauce is made from a concentration of oysters, soy sauce, and brine. Dark brown in color, it has a mild and sophisticated taste. The rich yet subtle and smooth taste helps to strengthen food flavors. Scrod is young cod. You may substitute flounder, pollack, or haddock.

4 Servings

Chili Oyster Sauce

- 1 teaspoon light soy sauce
- 3 tablespoons oyster sauce
- 2 tablespoons dry white wine
- ½ teaspoon fresh ginger, grated
- 2 cloves garlic, minced
- 1 teaspoon garlic chili sauce (available at oriental food stores)
- ½ teaspoon sugar

Scrod

- Canola oil, or non-stick cooking spray
- 2 cloves garlic
- ½ cup green onions, chopped
- 1 can (6½ ozs.) water chestnuts, drained, chopped
- 2 cups bok choy, chopped
- 1¼–1½ lbs. scrod fillets, cut into 4 servings

Chili Oyster Sauce: In small saucepan, mix together soy sauce, oyster sauce, wine, ginger, garlic, chili sauce, and sugar. Heat 1 minute, stirring occasionally. Set sauce aside until ready to use.

Scrod: Preheat oven to 375° F. Wash fish and pat dry.

Saute garlic and onions in sprayed frying pan 5 minutes or until soft and beginning to brown. Add water chestnuts and bok choy. Continue cooking about 4 minutes, stirring occasionally. Cook until water chestnuts are just crisp.

Spoon vegetable filling over each scrod fillet. Roll fish up jelly roll style. Set scrod in sprayed casserole pan, seam side down. Cover fish with parchment paper.

Bake fish 12 to 15 minutes or until just cooked. Fish is done when it becomes opaque and flakes easily. Remove fish with slotted spoon. Set each piece of fish on an individual plate, and spoon Chili Oyster Sauce over it. Good with hot brown or white rice.

Nutritional Data

PER SERVING		EXCHANGES	
Calories:	184	Milk:	0.0
Fat (gm):	1.0	Veg.:	1.0
Sat. fat (gm):	0.2	Fruit:	0.0
Cholesterol (mg):	56	Bread:	0.0
Sodium (mg):	339	Meat:	3.0
% Calories from fat:	5	Fat:	0.0

TERIYAKI BASS

Rather than soak the fish in marinade, we just brush it to give a rich taste when cooked. You can substitute bluefish, snapper, or haddock.

6 Servings

Bass

1½ lbs. sea bass fillets

Teriyaki Marinade

¼ cup light soy sauce

1 teaspoon sugar

2 tablespoons sake, or dry white wine

2 cloves garlic, minced

½ teaspoon fresh ginger, grated

¼ teaspoon red pepper flakes

Canola oil, or non-stick cooking spray

Bass: Cut fish into 1-inch pieces and place on a plate.

Teriyaki Marinade: Combine all ingredients in small bowl. Brush fish with marinade on both sides. Let stand for 20 minutes.

Arrange fish pieces on sprayed broiling pan. Broil fish about 6 inches from heat for 7 to 8 minutes or until it flakes easily when tested with fork.

Transfer fish to warm serving platter and serve immediately.

Nutritional Data

PER SERVING		EXCHANGES	
Calories:	124	Milk:	0.0
Fat (gm):	2.3	Veg.:	0.0
Sat. fat (gm):	0.6	Fruit:	0.0
Cholesterol (mg):	47	Bread:	0.0
Sodium (mg):	448	Meat:	2.5
% Calories from fat:	15	Fat:	0.0

PAN FRIED BASS WITH PICKLED BEETS

Pickled beets make a spicy and interesting side dish to accompany fish. They can be prepared days before serving and allowed to mellow in the refrigerator. This is especially good in the fall when farmers' markets are brimming with fresh beets. You can prepare it with canned beets, but for better results use fresh.

6 Servings

Pickled Beets

1½ lbs. beets, washed, skin on
¼ cup red wine vinegar
2 teaspoons sugar
1 teaspoon caraway seeds
1½ teaspoons prepared horseradish

Bass

1½ lbs. sea bass fillets, cut into 1-in. pieces
  Olive oil, or non-stick cooking spray
⅓ cup fine rye breadcrumbs
½ teaspoon rosemary
¼ teaspoon white pepper

Pickled Beets: Scrub and trim beets. Place them in pot, cover with water, and cook in skins until tender. Cool and drain. Peel beets and cut into thin slices.

Place beet slices in glass jar and add remaining pickling ingredients. Toss beets. Cover lightly and refrigerate 24 hours before serving.

Bass: Spray a non-stick frying pan. Toss breadcrumbs with rosemary and white pepper. Roll fish pieces in breadcrumbs. Cook fish over medium-high heat on both sides until cooked. Fish is done when it is opaque and just firm to the touch.

Remove fish to individual plates. Spoon ⅓ cup of Pickled Beets onto each plate. Serve extra beets at the table for guests to help themselves.

Nutritional Data

PER SERVING		EXCHANGES	
Calories:	163	Milk:	0.0
Fat (gm):	2.6	Veg.:	2.0
Sat. fat (gm):	0.6	Fruit:	0.0
Cholesterol (mg):	47	Bread:	0.0
Sodium (mg):	171	Meat:	2.0
% Calories from fat:	15	Fat:	0.0

MICROWAVE BASS WITH PARSLEY AND LIME PEEL

You can substitute grouper or cod for black sea bass. This fish is from the Atlantic, ranging from Maine all the way south to the Gulf of Mexico.

4 Servings

Parsley and Lime Peel

2 cups parsley, minced

4 large garlic cloves, minced

¾ cup red onions, minced

3 tablespoons lime peel

Bass

1¼–1½ lbs. black sea bass fillets, cut into 4 portions

1 small red onion, sliced

1 cup celery, thinly sliced

½ teaspoon celery seeds

Parsley and Lime Peel: In a bowl, mix parsley, garlic, onions, and lime peel. Set aside until serving time.

Bass: Wash fish and pat dry. Put red onion and celery slices on bottom of a glass pie plate or other dish suitable for microwave oven. Arrange fish on top, making sure that the thickness of the fish is even. Tuck thin end pieces under thicker parts of the fillets. Sprinkle fish with celery seeds. Cover plate securely with plastic wrap suitable for microwave. Cook 3–4 minutes on High or until fish is done. Fish is cooked when it is opaque and will flake easily when prodded with fork. Remove plastic wrap carefully so as not to be affected by the steam. Drain off excess liquid.

Toss parsley mixture again and arrange it on bottom of a serving platter. Using a slotted spoon or spatula, remove fish pieces and place them over parsley mixture.

Nutritional Data

PER SERVING		EXCHANGES	
Calories:	184	Milk:	0.0
Fat (gm):	3.2	Veg.:	1.0
Sat. fat (gm):	0.8	Fruit:	0.0
Cholesterol (mg):	59	Bread:	0.0
Sodium (mg):	138	Meat:	3.0
% Calories from fat:	16	Fat:	0.0

MAHIMAHI WITH SHALLOTS AND MUSHROOMS

Red sea bass, snapper, and yellowtail can all be substituted for mahimahi.

6 Servings

Olive oil, or non-stick cooking spray
1 teaspoon margarine
2 cloves garlic, minced
½ cup shallots, minced
1 lb. brown or white mushrooms, trimmed, cleaned, sliced
3 tablespoons dry red wine
½ teaspoon each: rosemary; basil
¼ teaspoon black pepper, freshly ground
1¼–1½ lbs. mahimahi fillets, cut into serving-size pieces
¼ cup tomato juice

To prepare shallot and mushroom mixture, spray a non-stick frying pan and melt margarine. Saute garlic and shallots 5 minutes over medium heat, stirring occasionally. Stir in mushrooms, wine, rosemary, basil, and freshly ground black pepper. Continue cooking, stirring occasionally, until mushrooms are cooked; they will be soft and tender. Set aside.

Place fish in baking dish and drizzle with tomato juice. Preheat oven to 375° F. Bake fish about 15 minutes or until cooked to taste. Fish should be opaque and flake easily when prodded with fork.

To serve, set a piece of fish on each plate and spoon hot shallot and mushroom mixture over top.

Nutritional Data

PER SERVING		EXCHANGES	
Calories:	105	Milk:	0.0
Fat (gm):	1.2	Veg.:	0.0
Sat. fat (gm):	0.2	Fruit:	0.0
Cholesterol (mg):	55	Bread:	0.0
Sodium (mg):	115	Meat:	2.0
% Calories from fat:	10	Fat:	0.0

MAHIMAHI WITH GREEN SAUCE

All medium-thick and thicker fish are suitable for baking.

4 Servings

Green Sauce

  Olive oil, or non-stick cooking spray
2 cloves garlic, minced
1 shallot, minced
½ cup parsley, minced
¼ teaspoon each: pepper; thyme; marjoram
2 tablespoons dry white wine

Mahimahi

1¼–1½ lbs. mahimahi fillets, cut into 4 serving-size
   pieces
4 teaspoons balsamic vinegar
  Double-thickness aluminum foil

Green Sauce: Spray saucepan with oil. Saute garlic and shallot about 3 minutes, stirring occasionally over medium heat. Add parsley, pepper, thyme, marjoram, and wine. Stir well and remove from heat.

Mahimahi: Sprinkle fish with balsamic vinegar. Wrap each piece in foil. Seal foil, envelope style, and place on cookie sheet. Preheat oven to 375° F. Bake fish 15 minutes or until done. To check for doneness, open one package. Fish is done when it is opaque and flakes easily when prodded with fork.

Partially open each fish packet and sprinkle with Green Sauce. Serve fish in the packages. Good with boiled new potatoes.

Nutritional Data

PER SERVING		EXCHANGES	
Calories:	114	Milk:	0.0
Fat (gm):	0.9	Veg.:	0.0
Sat. fat (gm):	0.2	Fruit:	0.0
Cholesterol (mg):	83	Bread:	0.0
Sodium (mg):	104	Meat:	2.0
% Calories from fat:	7	Fat:	0.0

BROILED MAHIMAHI WITH MINT

If fresh mint is not available, use dried mint. Always wash and pat dry fish before cooking.

4 Servings

½ cup dry breadcrumbs
2 cloves garlic, minced
2 tablespoons fresh parsley, minced
2 tablespoons fresh mint, minced
¼ teaspoon white pepper
1¼–1½ lbs. mahimahi fillets

Mix together breadcrumbs, garlic, parsley, mint, and pepper. Set aside.

Wash and pat dry mahimahi fillets. Preheat oven to 375° F. Set fish on non-stick cookie sheet. Sprinkle flavored breadcrumbs over fish.

Bake fish 15 to 20 minutes. Turn fish if necessary, using spatula. Cook fish until done; it will be opaque and just firm to the touch. Remove to serving plate and serve hot.

Nutritional Data

PER SERVING		EXCHANGES	
Calories:	149	Milk:	0.0
Fat (gm):	1.4	Veg.:	0.0
Sat. fat (gm):	0.3	Fruit:	0.0
Cholesterol (mg):	83	Bread:	0.5
Sodium (mg):	192	Meat:	2.5
% Calories from fat:	9	Fat:	0.0

CATFISH NUGGETS WITH ORIENTAL LEMON SAUCE

Catfish nuggets are tender cuts of catfish fillets. As you may know, catfish is mostly farm-raised in the Midwest and California, affording the consumer a more stable product with consistency of flavor.

6 Servings

Catfish

1¼–1½ lbs. catfish nuggets
⅓ cup fine breadcrumbs
½ teaspoon ginger root, freshly grated
1 clove garlic, minced

Oriental Lemon Sauce

⅓ cup lemon juice, freshly squeezed
2 tablespoons lemon rind, freshly grated
1¼ cups chicken stock
2 tablespoons light brown sugar
½ teaspoon ginger root, freshly grated
2 tablespoons green onions, minced
2 teaspoons cornstarch

Catfish: Wash and pat dry catfish nuggets. Mix together breadcrumbs, ginger, and garlic. Sprinkle flavored crumbs over catfish and set fish on cookie sheet. Preheat oven to 375° F. Bake fish 10 to 15 minutes, turning once. Cook until fish is opaque and just firm to the touch.

Oriental Lemon Sauce: While fish is baking, in a small saucepan, combine all sauce ingredients except cornstarch. Cook over medium heat, stirring often, until sauce comes to a boil. Reduce heat to simmer and continue cooking 3 to 4 minutes. Remove ⅓ cup of sauce and stir cornstarch into it. Return cornstarch mixture to sauce and continue simmering. Sauce will thicken slightly. Stir sauce as it thickens.

When fish is cooked, spoon it into a bowl, drizzle Oriental Lemon Sauce over it, and serve hot. Good with whole-wheat oriental noodles.

Nutritional Data

PER SERVING		EXCHANGES	
Calories:	142	Milk:	0.0
Fat (gm):	3.8	Veg.:	0.0
Sat. fat (gm):	0.9	Fruit:	0.0
Cholesterol (mg):	43	Bread:	0.5
Sodium (mg):	252	Meat:	2.0
% Calories from fat:	25	Fat:	0.0

MICROWAVE CATFISH WITH SOUTHWEST SAUCE AND CORN RELISH

*Catfish is one of those fish that must be skinned before cooking.
See Chapter 2 for instructions.*

4 Servings

Southwest Brushing Sauce

- ½ cup beer
- ½ teaspoon liquid wood-smoke flavoring (optional)
- 2 tablespoons red wine vinegar
- 2 tablespoons dark brown sugar
- 2 cloves garlic, minced

Corn Relish

- 1 red bell pepper, seeded, chopped
- ½ cup canned corn niblets, drained
- 3 green onions, minced
- ⅛ teaspoon celery seeds
- 2 teaspoons lime juice, freshly squeezed
- 3 tablespoons cilantro, chopped

Catfish

- 1¼–1½ lbs. catfish fillets
- 1 red bell pepper, seeded, sliced
- ½ teaspoon chili powder

Southwest Sauce: Mix together all sauce ingredients in a small bowl. Brush catfish on both sides with sauce and let stand 30 minutes.

Corn Relish: In a glass bowl, combine peppers, corn, and onions. Mix in celery seeds, lime juice, and chopped cilantro. Cover lightly and refrigerate until serving time. Stir before serving.

Catfish: Using a microwave-safe dish, arrange bell pepper slices on bottom of dish. Brush fish again with sauce and sprinkle with chili powder. Place fish over pepper slices, tucking thinner ends under thicker so that fish is even. Cover dish securely with plastic wrap for the microwave, and cook 3 to 4 minutes. If fish is not cooked, continue cooking until fish is opaque and flakes easily when prodded with fork. Remove from microwave and remove wrap away from you to avoid escaping steam. Discard plastic wrap.

Serve fish hot, and spoon Corn Relish on the side.

Nutritional Data

PER SERVING		EXCHANGES	
Calories:	235	Milk:	0.0
Fat (gm):	6.4	Veg.:	1.0
Sat. fat (gm):	1.4	Fruit:	0.0
Cholesterol (mg):	82	Bread:	0.5
Sodium (mg):	163	Meat:	3.0
% Calories from fat:	24	Fat:	0.0

ORANGE ROUGHY GYPSY STYLE

It is the rich taste of Hungarian paprika that gives this fish and vegetable dish its name.

6 Servings

- 3 large potatoes, scrubbed, quartered
- 2 carrots, sliced
- 1½ lbs. orange roughy fillets, cut into 2-in. strips
- 2 red bell peppers, seeded, sliced
- 2 tomatoes, sliced
- ½ cup onions, chopped
- ½ cup non-fat plain yogurt
- ¼ teaspoon each: salt; pepper; Hungarian paprika (to taste)
- ¼ cup parsley, minced

C ook potatoes and carrots in lightly salted water until just tender, about 20 minutes; drain. Peel potatoes and slice. Spread potatoes and carrots over bottom of ovenproof baking dish.

Arrange fish strips over vegetables. Arrange peppers, tomatoes, and onions over fish. Mix yogurt with salt, pepper, and paprika, and spoon it over entire casserole.

Preheat oven to 375° F. Bake fish 10 to 15 minutes or until cooked; it should be opaque and just firm to the touch. Let casserole stand 5 minutes. Using a slotted spoon, arrange portions on individual dishes. Serve hot, sprinkled with parsley.

Nutritional Data

PER SERVING		EXCHANGES	
Calories:	214	Milk:	0.0
Fat (gm):	6.7	Veg.:	1.5
Sat. fat (gm):	0.2	Fruit:	0.0
Cholesterol (mg):	18	Bread:	1.0
Sodium (mg):	178	Meat:	2.0
% Calories from fat:	28	Fat:	0.0

ORANGE ROUGHY WITH CELERIAC SALAD

Celeriac, or celery root, is just what you think it is by its name, that is, a root vegetable with a strong celery flavor. It is an ugly looking root, but when trimmed and peeled, it becomes a delicious vegetable. Celeriac is usually grated and used in salads. Remember that it discolors easily and should be refreshed with lemon juice.

6 Servings

Celeriac Salad

- ¾ lb. celeriac, trimmed, peeled, grated
- 2 tablespoons lemon juice, freshly squeezed
- 2 tablespoons red wine vinegar
- 2 tablespoons fat-free mayonnaise
- 2 teaspoons stone-ground mustard
- 1 teaspoon tarragon
- ½ teaspoon caraway seeds
- ¼ teaspoon each: salt; pepper
- 1 cup breadcrumbs

Orange Roughy

- 1 lb. orange roughy fillets, cut into 2-in. strips
- Olive oil, or non-stick cooking spray
- ½ cup red onions, chopped
- ¼ cup shallots, minced
- ¼ teaspoon white pepper
- 1 tablespoon lemon rind, freshly grated

Celeriac Salad: Grate the celeriac and toss with lemon juice in glass bowl. Mix in remaining salad ingredients. Taste to adjust seasonings. Cover lightly and refrigerate until ready to serve. Sprinkle with breadcrumbs and toss before serving.

Orange Roughy: Wash fish and pat dry. Set aside. Spray a non-stick frying pan and saute onions and shallots until tender, stirring occasionally. Add fish strips and gently pan fry on both sides. Fish will brown slightly. Use a spatula to turn fish and keep pieces from breaking up. Sprinkle with white pepper and lemon rind.

Serve fish hot with Celeriac Salad.

Nutritional Data

PER SERVING		EXCHANGES	
Calories:	193	Milk:	0.0
Fat (gm):	6.3	Veg.:	1.0
Sat. fat (gm):	0.3	Fruit:	0.0
Cholesterol (mg):	15	Bread:	1.0
Sodium (mg):	368	Meat:	2.0
% Calories from fat:	29	Fat:	0.0

MICROWAVE ORANGE ROUGHY WITH PORT SAUCE

4 Servings

Port Sauce

  Olive oil, or non-stick cooking spray

3 green onions, minced

1½ cups non-fat lemon yogurt

1 tablespoon lemon rind

3 tablespoons port

⅛ teaspoon each: white pepper; tarragon

Orange Roughy

1¼–1½ lbs. orange roughy fillets, cut into 4 serving pieces

2 tablespoons port

2 tablespoons chives, minced

Port Sauce: Spray a small non-stick frying pan and saute green onions, until tender, over medium heat, stirring occasionally. Remove from heat and transfer to a small bowl. Spoon in yogurt, lemon rind, and port. Stir in pepper and tarragon. Cover and refrigerate until serving time.

Orange Roughy: Spray a microwave-safe dish, and arrange fish with thin ends, if necessary, tucked under thicker ends to make fish even. Sprinkle fish with port and chives. Cover securely with plastic wrap for the microwave. Microwave 3 to 4 minutes on High. If fish is not cooked, continue cooking until it is opaque and flakes easily when prodded with fork. Remove from microwave and discard plastic wrap. (Remove wrap away from you to avoid escaping steam.)

Serve fish with a dollop of Port Sauce. Good with linguine.

Nutritional Data

PER SERVING		EXCHANGES	
Calories:	212	Milk:	1.0
Fat (gm):	1.5	Veg.:	0.0
Sat. fat (gm):	0.3	Fruit:	0.0
Cholesterol (mg):	54	Bread:	0.0
Sodium (mg):	112	Meat:	3.0
% Calories from fat:	6	Fat:	0.0

GRILLED ROCKFISH WITH SWEET-AND-SOUR SAUCE

There are many species of rockfish, all from the Pacific. Rockfish is a firm, colorful, snapper-like fish, and it is easy to cook.

6 Servings

Grilled Rockfish

1¼–1½ lbs. rockfish fillets (substitute red snapper if necessary)
  ½ cup plain non-fat yogurt
  2 tablespoons honey mustard
  ½ teaspoon chili powder
  3 red or green bell peppers, cut in half, seeded

Sweet-and-Sour Sauce

  ¾ cup plain non-fat yogurt
  ¼ cup red wine vinegar
  2 tablespoons dark brown sugar
  2 tablespoons catsup
  ¼ teaspoon each: Worcestershire sauce; honey mustard; curry powder
  2 cloves garlic, minced

Grilled Rockfish: Set fish on shallow plate. Mix together yogurt, mustard, and chili powder and brush onto fish fillets. Let fish marinate 45 minutes to 1 hour. Turn fish once and brush again while marinating.

When coals are hot, grill fish fillets and peppers on the barbecue 2 to 4 minutes. Turn fish and peppers over and grill a bit longer until done to taste. Remember not to overcook the fish. Fish will turn opaque when done and be just firm to the touch. Peppers will char when done; slice. Remove fish to a platter.

Sweet-and-Sour Sauce: Quickly, in a small bowl, stir together all sauce ingredients. Taste to adjust seasonings. Spoon a dollop of Sweet-and-Sour Sauce beside the fish. Serve hot.

Nutritional Data

PER SERVING		EXCHANGES	
Calories:	156	Milk:	0.5
Fat (gm):	2.0	Veg.:	0.0
Sat. fat (gm):	0.4	Fruit:	0.0
Cholesterol (mg):	33	Bread:	0.0
Sodium (mg):	225	Meat:	2.0
% Calories from fat:	12	Fat:	0.0

POACHED FISH FILLETS WITH LEEKS

This recipe can be prepared with fresh or thawed frozen fish. To thaw frozen fish, it is best to defrost it in the refrigerator.

4 Servings

½ cup onions, sliced
½ cup carrots, sliced
½ cup celery, sliced
1 clove garlic, crushed
½ cup dry white wine
1 lime, sliced
3 bay leaves
½ teaspoon thyme
1¼–1½ lbs. thawed or fresh fish fillets, such as bass, haddock, cod, or salmon
5 cups leeks, cleaned, sliced
Olive oil, or non-stick cooking spray
¼ teaspoon each: salt; pepper
½ teaspoon celery seeds

U se a fish poacher or other pan, such as a frying pan, filled three-quarters full with water. Add first 8 ingredients. Bring mixture to a boil. Reduce to simmer and continue cooking 8 to 10 minutes.

Set fish on a rack in poacher or pan, and cover with tight-fitting lid. Again bring liquid to a boil and reduce it to simmer. Continue cooking about 5 minutes or until fish is cooked. Fish will turn opaque and flake easily. Let fish remain in poaching liquid 8 to 10 minutes.

While fish is poaching, saute leeks in sprayed, non-stick frying pan until wilted, stirring often. Season with salt, pepper, and celery seeds. Taste to adjust seasonings.

With a slotted spoon, carefully remove fish and place on serving dish. Surround fish with warm leeks.

Nutritional Data

PER SERVING		EXCHANGES	
Calories:	232	Milk:	0.0
Fat (gm):	3.3	Veg.:	3.0
Sat. fat (gm):	0.8	Fruit:	0.0
Cholesterol (mg):	59	Bread:	0.0
Sodium (mg):	261	Meat:	3.0
% Calories from fat:	13	Fat:	0.0

FISH HASH AND LEEK PIZZA

This is a good use for leftover fish. Or buy fish when it is on sale or plentiful, and prepare a double batch, reserving the second batch of cooked fish for topping this pizza.

12 Servings

Whole-Wheat Crust
- 1 package dry yeast
- 1 cup warm water
- ½ teaspoon fennel seeds
- 1 tablespoon olive oil, optional
- 1¾ cups all-purpose flour
- 1 cup whole-wheat flour
- Olive oil, or non-stick cooking spray

Pizza Topping
- 1½ cups red onions, minced
- 1½ cups cooked potatoes, cubed
- 2 cups cooked fish, flaked
- ½ teaspoon each: fennel seeds; garlic powder; tarragon
- ¼ teaspoon white pepper
- 2 cups leeks, well cleaned, thinly sliced
- 3 cloves garlic, minced

Whole-Wheat Crust: Early in the day prepare the crust. Dissolve yeast in warm water. Stir fennel seeds and olive oil with the flours. Mix in the yeast. It is easy and convenient to prepare the crust in a food processor fitted with a steel blade.

Turn the dough out onto a lightly floured board, and knead until smooth. Place dough in ungreased bowl, cover lightly, and let rise until double in bulk, about 1 hour. Punch dough down and press with heel of your hand, or use a small rolling pin, spreading dough onto a 9 × 12-inch cookie sheet or pizza pan that has been sprayed with oil. Set aside. Dough can be covered and refrigerated at this point.

Pizza Topping: While dough is rising prepare topping. Spray a non-stick frying pan and saute onions and potatoes over medium heat until tender, stirring occasionally. Mix in fish and spices. Cook only until warm. Set aside.

Separately cook leeks. Spray a non-stick frying pan and saute leeks and garlic until tender, stirring occasionally, over medium heat. Set aside.

To assemble pizza, spread leeks over crust. Sprinkle the fish hash over leeks.

Preheat oven to 425° F. Place pizza on pizza tile or stone, and bake 20 minutes or until done to taste. Pizza is done when crust is golden and topping is hot. Serve immediately.

Nutritional Data

PER SERVING		EXCHANGES	
Calories:	167	Milk:	0.0
Fat (gm):	1.8	Veg.:	1.0
Sat. fat (gm):	0.3	Fruit:	0.0
Cholesterol (mg):	10	Bread:	1.5
Sodium (mg):	21	Meat:	0.5
% Calories from fat:	9	Fat:	0.0

FISH-FRIED RICE

If you are making this recipe from scratch, use a half-pound of any firm-fleshed fish or tiny shrimp. Otherwise, try this for a new twist on what to do with leftover fish. Serve it as a main dish or an accompaniment.

6 Servings

Canola oil, or non-stick cooking spray
⅓ cup green onions, chopped
1 onion, minced
1 cup oriental mushrooms, sliced, reconstituted
1 can (6½ ozs.) water chestnuts, minced
1 cup cooked fish or shrimp, flaked
2 cups cooked rice
½ cup defrosted or fresh peas
1 tablespoon light soy sauce
¼ teaspoon each: garlic powder; pepper
3 egg whites, slightly beaten

S pray a wok or non-stick frying pan with oil. Stir-fry onions until tender, 3 to 4 minutes. Add mushrooms, water chestnuts, and bits of cooked fish or baby shrimp. Continue stir-frying over high heat about 1 minute. Stir in rice and continue cooking until rice is separated and heated. Stir in peas, soy sauce, garlic powder, pepper, and egg whites. Stir-fry until egg whites have been absorbed. Taste to adjust seasonings. Serve hot.

Nutritional Data

PER SERVING		EXCHANGES	
Calories:	170	Milk:	0.0
Fat (gm):	0.5	Veg.:	2.0
Sat. fat (gm):	0.1	Fruit:	0.0
Cholesterol (mg):	7	Bread:	1.0
Sodium (mg):	149	Meat:	1.0
% Calories from fat:	3	Fat:	0.0

5.
THICKER FISH

Tuna
Salmon
Swordfish
Shark
Grouper
Finnan Haddie

Tuna Veracruz

Veracruz style refers to baking a firm fish with tomatoes, potatoes, lime juice, olives, and capers. It is an easy party dish. Instead of the traditional whole fish, I have substituted tuna steaks.

6 Servings

- 2 lbs. fresh tuna steaks, cut into 6 portions
  Juice from 1 lime
- ¼ cup olive oil
- 1 large onion, sliced
- 2 cloves garlic, minced
- 2 lbs. tomatoes, peeled, seeded, chopped
- 6 medium potatoes, cooked, peeled, sliced
- 2 medium red bell peppers, seeded, cut into strips
- 3 bay leaves
- ½ teaspoon each: oregano; cumin; cayenne
- ½ cup stuffed green olives
- 4 tablespoons capers, including juice

 prinkle tuna steaks with lime juice. Set aside. Preheat oven to 400° F.

Heat oil in frying pan over medium heat. Saute onion and garlic until soft, about 5 minutes, stirring occasionally. Add tomatoes, potatoes, peppers, bay leaves, and spices. Simmer sauce for 10 minutes, covered.

Set fish in a shallow, ovenproof dish. Cover with sauce and sprinkle with olives and capers. Bake until fish flakes easily and is just firm to the touch, 10 to 12 minutes, depending on thickness of fish. Do not over-cook. Discard bay leaves.

Remove fish with slotted spoon to serving dishes. Spoon sauce over fish. Serve hot. Good with Mexican beer and nacho chips.

Nutritional Data

PER SERVING		EXCHANGES	
Calories:	381	Milk:	0.0
Fat (gm):	11.5	Veg.:	2.0
Sat. fat (gm):	1.7	Fruit:	0.0
Cholesterol (mg):	54	Bread:	1.0
Sodium (mg):	174	Meat:	4.0
% Calories from fat:	27	Fat:	1.0

GRILLED TUNA STEAKS WITH PEPPERS AND ELEPHANT GARLIC

Aristotle was the first person to write about Mediterranean tuna. It is a rich, full-bodied fish. For best results, it should be cooked lightly and remain pink in the center. This recipe calls for "elephant" garlic, which simply is a very large clove of garlic. When it is baked or grilled, garlic takes on an almost nutty flavor and becomes somewhat mild tasting. Try it and be pleasantly surprised.

6 Servings

Tuna

1¼–1½ lbs. tuna steaks, cut into 6 serving-size portions

Marinade

1 tablespoon extra virgin olive oil
3 tablespoons red wine vinegar
¼ cup each: chopped onions; chopped parsley

Accompaniments

6 cloves elephant garlic, peeled, wrapped in aluminum foil
Canola oil, or non-stick cooking spray
3 red bell peppers, seeded, cut into 1½-in. slices

Tuna: Cut into serving-size portions and put in large plastic self-sealing bag.

Marinade: Combine all ingredients. Pour marinade in bag with tuna steaks. Set bag in pie plate or shallow glass dish and let stand at room temperature 1 hour. Turn bag several times so that all areas of fish are touched by marinade. Be sure that bag is sealed securely. Drain.

Accompaniments: Arrange elephant garlic on preheated grill, as it will take 15 to 20 minutes to cook. Garlic is done when it is tender. Turn foil-wrapped garlic every 5 minutes.

Place tuna steaks on sprayed grill rack and set over hot coals. Grill fish 4 to 5 minutes, turning every 2 minutes until fish is done to taste. Grill pepper strips at the same time that you grill fish, 2 to 4 minutes or until done. Peppers will char.

Serve tuna hot with garlic and red peppers. Instruct guests to spread garlic over tuna.

Nutritional Data

PER SERVING		EXCHANGES	
Calories:	110	Milk:	0.0
Fat (gm):	2.3	Veg.:	0.0
Sat. fat (gm):	0.4	Fruit:	0.0
Cholesterol (mg):	34	Bread:	0.0
Sodium (mg):	29	Meat:	2.0
% Calories from fat:	19	Fat:	0.0

TUNA KABOBS WITH FRUIT

Tuna is fished on both coasts. The fish varies in color from white, the albacore, to a reddish color with purple tints. Tuna can vary in size from 8 or 10 pounds to 600 or 700 pounds. Once while visiting in a coastal town in Maine, we watched fishermen hoist ashore a 650-pound tuna. The fish is best served as steaks or in chunks for kabobs.

4 Servings

Lime Juice Brushing Sauce
　　Juice from 2 limes
　3　cloves garlic, smashed
　¼　cup rice-wine vinegar
　¼　teaspoon pepper

Tuna
　1¼　lbs. tuna steak, cut into 1-in. pieces

Fruit
　16　fresh or dried figs, soaked in ½ cup sweet red wine, drained
　2　large bananas, peeled, cut into 1½-in. pieces
　1　tablespoon dark brown sugar
　1　lime, sliced
　4　long double-pronged skewers, or bamboo skewers soaked in water 30 minutes and drained

Lime Juice Brushing Sauce: Combine ingredients in small glass bowl.

Tuna: Place tuna pieces in single layer in glass dish such as a quiche pan or pie plate. Brush tuna with sauce. Let fish stand 45 minutes before threading it onto skewers. Drain.

Fruit: Thread skewers, alternating tuna pieces with figs and banana chunks sprinkled with brown sugar. Thread a lime slice at the end of each kabob.

Preheat broiler. Place kabobs on broiler rack and broil 3 minutes; turn and cook another 3 to 6 minutes or until done. Fish will turn opaque and fruit will char slightly. Set skewers on plates and serve hot.

Nutritional Data

PER SERVING		EXCHANGES	
Calories:	388	Milk:	0.0
Fat (gm):	2.3	Veg.:	0.0
Sat. fat (gm):	0.6	Fruit:	3.0
Cholesterol (mg):	64	Bread:	0.0
Sodium (mg):	58	Meat:	4.0
% Calories from fat:	5	Fat:	0.0

POACHED SALMON WITH ORIENTAL VEGETABLES

◆

Most fish can be poached, but thick, firm fillets are best. This cooking technique involves simmering the fish, below the boiling point, usually in a seasoned liquid. There is a special poaching pan, elongated and designed just for this method of cooking. But it is easy to improvise by using a wok, large kettle, pot, or roasting pan. I remember my grandmother using a soup pot, with the fish wrapped in cheesecloth and suspended from the handles. It worked! Cover the pot while poaching. After poaching, drain off the liquid and discard the fish skin. Fish most suitable for poaching include salmon, cod, haddock, halibut, trout, and whitefish.

6 Servings

2–2½	lbs. salmon fillets
1	cup dry white wine
1	tablespoon lime juice, freshly squeezed
½	cup onions, sliced
½	teaspoon each: pepper; tarragon
	Canola oil, or non-stick spray
2	cloves garlic, minced
½	teaspoon fresh ginger root, minced
3	cups bok choy, sliced
1	cup snow peas, trimmed
¼	cup fish stock
¼	teaspoon red pepper flakes
1	teaspoon light soy sauce
1	tablespoon cornstarch mixed with 2 tablespoons water

Run fingers over salmon to remove any bones. Fill poacher with enough water to cover fish when added. Add wine, juice, onions, and spices. Bring liquid to a boil. Lower heat; simmer 5 minutes. Place fish on poaching rack (it should be covered with liquid) and cover. Poach 10 minutes or until salmon is cooked. Salmon is done when it becomes a brighter opaque color, is slightly firm to the touch, and flakes easily when prodded with fork. Let stand in liquid 5 minutes. Transfer salmon to a platter and cool.

While fish is cooling, prepare vegetables in sprayed wok or heavy frying pan. Saute garlic and ginger over high heat until beginning to color. Add bok choy and peas and stir-fry about 5 minutes or until cooked but still crisp. Stir in remaining ingredients. Continue cooking 1 to 2 minutes or until sauce thickens slightly.

Arrange vegetables around fish and bring to the table.

Nutritional Data

PER SERVING		EXCHANGES	
Calories:	319	Milk:	0.0
Fat (gm):	9.4	Veg.:	2.0
Sat. fat (gm):	1.8	Fruit:	0.0
Cholesterol (mg):	59	Bread:	0.0
Sodium (mg):	217	Meat:	5.0
% Calories from fat:	27	Fat:	0.0

CARPACCIO OF SALMON

This must be made with only the freshest fish and served quickly. Adapted from the Italian, it is very easy to prepare and delicious. Serve with toast.

4 Servings

½ lb. center cut piece of freshest salmon (tell your fishmonger that fish is to be eaten raw and must be exceptionally fresh)

1 teaspoon best quality olive oil

¼ teaspoon black pepper, freshly ground

3 tablespoons capers

⅓ cup parsley, minced

⅓ cup cilantro, minced

1 lemon, sliced

6 slices dark rye, toasted, cut into quarters

Slice salmon into paper-thin pieces. Arrange 3 slices on each of 4 chilled salad plates. Drizzle olive oil over salmon and sprinkle with freshly ground pepper. Sprinkle with capers and their brine. Sprinkle parsley and cilantro over carpaccio.

Serve carpaccio as a first course or luncheon dish. Present it chilled with lemon slices and toasted rye bread.

Nutritional Data

PER SERVING		EXCHANGES	
Calories:	192	Milk:	0.0
Fat (gm):	6.2	Veg.:	0.0
Sat. fat (gm):	0.7	Fruit:	0.0
Cholesterol (mg):	31	Bread:	1.5
Sodium (mg):	290	Meat:	1.5
% Calories from fat:	29	Fat:	0.0

SWORDFISH KABOBS WITH EGGPLANT AND ZUCCHINI

Swordfish is a firm, tasty, rich-flavored fish. This fish tends to be dry if overcooked, so watch that it doesn't dry out. Swordfish is caught on both the Pacific and Atlantic coasts. Double-pronged skewers are just what the name implies: a fork-like cooking tool that keeps fish and vegetables steady so that they do not roll around on the skewer. They are available at large department and cookware stores.

4 Servings

Swordfish

1¼–1½ lbs. swordfish steaks, cut into 1-in. pieces

Sage-Rosemary Marinade

⅓ cup freshly squeezed lemon juice

1 teaspoon olive oil

½ teaspoon each ingredient: sage, rosemary

2 cloves garlic, minced

Vegetables

1 medium eggplant, peeled, cut into 1-in. cubes

2 medium-small zucchini, cut into ¾-in. slices

1 large tomato, cut into eighths

1 large red onion, cut into quarters

4 double-pronged skewers, or bamboo skewers soaked in water 10 minutes and drained

Swordfish: Put fish in large plastic bag.

Marinade: Mix all ingredients together and pour into fish bag. Seal securely and place in shallow bowl to marinate 1 hour. Turn bag several times so that all areas of fish are touched by marinade.

Vegetables: Thread fish and vegetables alternately onto skewers. Reserve marinade to brush the vegetables. You might want to use 4 sage leaves, if available, to thread at the end of each skewer.

Preheat grill, using hardwood charcoal, until coals are hot. Grill kabobs 8 to 10 minutes, rotating them every 3 minutes. Fish will turn opaque and vegetables will char slightly.

Remove skewers to individual plates and serve hot.

Nutritional Data

PER SERVING		EXCHANGES	
Calories:	227	Milk:	0.0
Fat (gm):	7.1	Veg.:	1.5
Sat. fat (gm):	1.8	Fruit:	0.0
Cholesterol (mg):	56	Bread:	0.0
Sodium (mg):	134	Meat:	3.5
% Calories from fat:	28	Fat:	0.0

ITALIAN-SPICED SWORDFISH KABOBS WITH SQUASH

The history of kabobs is traced to the Middle East region. How it started is not clear; maybe a Persian soldier thought of putting chunks of meat on his sword to roast over a campfire. The word "kabob" means roasted meat. In the Middle East you still find traditional kabobs served in restaurants and homes.

4 Servings

- 1¼ lbs. swordfish, cut into 1-in. pieces
- ⅓ cup low-calorie Italian salad dressing
- ¼ teaspoon each: basil; oregano
- 12 pattypan squash, partially cooked (cook squash in water that has been brought to a boil and reduced to medium until squash is almost fork-tender, drain and cool)
- 2 medium-small zucchini, cut into ¾-in. pieces
- 1 onion, cut into quarters
- 4 double-pronged skewers, or bamboo skewers soaked in water 30 minutes and drained

Put swordfish in shallow glass dish in a single layer. Drizzle swordfish with salad dressing and sprinkle with basil and oregano. Let fish stand 45 minutes before threading onto kabobs. Drain fish. Reserve remaining dressing to brush vegetables.

Preheat broiler. Thread swordfish pieces onto skewers alternately with squash, zucchini, and onions. Brush vegetables with remaining dressing.

Set kabobs on broiler rack, about 6 inches from heat source, and broil 3 minutes; turn and cook another 3 minutes or until fish is done to taste. Remember not to overcook fish. Fish is done when it turns opaque and flakes easily when prodded with fork. Serve hot.

Nutritional Data

PER SERVING		EXCHANGES	
Calories:	248	Milk:	0.0
Fat (gm):	7.9	Veg.:	3.0
Sat. fat (gm):	1.9	Fruit:	0.0
Cholesterol (mg):	57	Bread:	0.0
Sodium (mg):	291	Meat:	3.0
% Calories from fat:	29	Fat:	0.0

GRILLED SWORDFISH WITH CHILI-LIME SAUCE

Swordfish works well on the grill. The flesh is firm and opaque when cooked. You can substitute snapper if swordfish is not available. For hardwood charcoal and aromatic flavoring send to People's Gourmet Woods, 55 Mill Street, Cumberland, RI 02864; (401) 715-2700.

6 Servings

Swordfish

1¼–1½ lbs. swordfish, cut into serving-size pieces
3 pieces apple wood, hickory, plum wood, or aromatic woods or chips of your choice

Brushing Sauce

1 teaspoon olive oil
2 tablespoons lime juice, freshly squeezed
¼ teaspoon pepper
2 tablespoons parsley, minced

Chili-Lime Sauce

¼ cup chili sauce
2 cups tomatoes, chopped
2 jalapeño peppers, seeded, chopped (use rubber gloves when preparing jalapeño peppers)
   Juice of ½ lime

Swordfish: Cut into serving-size pieces and place on a plate.

Brushing Sauce: Mix together olive oil, juice, pepper, and parsley. Brush swordfish with sauce. Let stand 1 hour.

Chili-Lime Sauce: In small bowl, mix together chili sauce, tomatoes, peppers, and juice. Set aside.

When coals are hot, grill fish on sprayed grill rack. Cook 4 to 6 minutes, then turn fish with long-handled spatula and continue cooking until done. The time will depend on thickness of fish and heat of coals. Remember not to overcook fish.

Remove fish to individual dishes, and spoon Chili-Lime Sauce over it. Serve hot.

Nutritional Data

PER SERVING		EXCHANGES	
Calories:	151	Milk:	0.0
Fat (gm):	4.8	Veg.:	1.0
Sat. fat (gm):	1.2	Fruit:	0.0
Cholesterol (mg):	37	Bread:	0.0
Sodium (mg):	310	Meat:	2.5
% Calories from fat:	29	Fat:	0.0

MARGARITA SWORDFISH

For those of you who enjoy the combination of tequila and fresh-squeezed lime juice, we suggest the following recipe.

6 Servings

Margarita Marinade
  1 cup lime juice, freshly squeezed
  1½ tablespoons tequila
  ¼ teaspoon salt

Swordfish
1¼–1½ lbs. swordfish, cut into 6 serving pieces
  12 corn husks (outer green husks), soaked in
      water 30 minutes, drained
  12 long chives

Margarita Marinade: Combine lime juice, tequila, and salt in bowl.
Swordfish: Put fish in large self-sealing bag and add marinade.
Seal bag securely and turn it several times so all surfaces of fish are
touched by marinade. Set bag in shallow dish and marinate in refrigerator 2 hours, turning once. Drain.
  Place each piece of fish into the natural curve of a corn husk. Cover
it with another corn husk. Turn bottom and top under, making a neat
package, resembling a tamale. Tie each with chives.
  To steam fish, set packages on a steamer rack (or inverted dish in a
steamer), bring water to a boil, and reduce to simmer. Cover steamer
and cook 8 to 12 minutes or until done to taste. Open one package to see
if fish is done. Fish will flake easily when cooked and be slightly firm to
the touch.
  Using a slotted spoon, transfer packages to individual plates. Allow
guests to open each. Serve hot. Good with Mexican rice, beans, and
salsa.

Nutritional Data

PER SERVING		EXCHANGES	
Calories:	121	Milk:	0.0
Fat (gm):	3.8	Veg.:	0.0
Sat. fat (gm):	1.0	Fruit:	0.0
Cholesterol (mg):	37	Bread:	0.0
Sodium (mg):	114	Meat:	2.0
% Calories from fat:	29	Fat:	0.0

Microwave Barbecued Swordfish

The swordfish ranges in temperate to warm waters around the world. This fish can grow in length to 12 or 13 feet. The meat is thick and tasty and usually cut into steaks.

4 Servings

Barbecue Sauce

	Canola oil, or non-stick cooking spray
2	cloves garlic, minced
½	cup onions, chopped
¼	cup catsup
2	cups tomatoes, peeled, seeded, chopped
¼	cup chili sauce
2	tablespoons dark brown sugar
1	teaspoon chili powder
½	teaspoon Worcestershire sauce
¼	teaspoon each: cumin; pepper

Swordfish

1	tomato, sliced
2	jalapeño peppers, seeded, chopped (wear rubber gloves when preparing jalapeño peppers and avoid touching your eyes)
1¼–1½	lbs. swordfish steaks, cut into 4 serving pieces
½	teaspoon cumin seeds

Barbecue Sauce: Spray saucepan and saute garlic and onions until tender, 4 to 5 minutes, over medium heat, stirring occasionally. Mix in catsup, tomatoes, chili sauce, sugar, chili powder, Worcestershire sauce, cumin, and pepper. Bring sauce to a boil; reduce heat to simmer. Continue cooking 15 minutes. Cool. Pour sauce into a container, cover, and refrigerate until ready to serve. Stir before serving.

Swordfish: Spray a microwave-safe glass dish, such as a glass pie plate, and arrange tomato slices on bottom sprinkled with chopped peppers. Set swordfish steaks atop vegetables and sprinkle with cumin seeds. Cover dish securely with plastic wrap for the microwave. Microwave on High for 2 minutes; turn over and microwave another 2 minutes or until done. Fish is done when it is opaque and flakes easily when prodded with fork. Drain off excessive liquid.

Remove from microwave and carefully take off plastic wrap, allowing steam to escape away from you. Using a spatula, remove tomato, peppers, and fish to individual plates. Drizzle 2 tablespoons of Barbecue Sauce over the swordfish. Serve hot.

Nutritional Data

PER SERVING		EXCHANGES	
Calories:	260	Milk:	0.0
Fat (gm):	6.1	Veg.:	3.0
Sat. fat (gm):	1.6	Fruit:	0.0
Cholesterol (mg):	56	Bread:	0.0
Sodium (mg):	586	Meat:	3.0
% Calories from fat:	21	Fat:	0.0

BAKED SHARK WITH HOISIN SAUCE

Hoisin sauce is a bean-based oriental sauce. Rich, thick, and brown, it glistens as it is poured from a bottle or can. It is a special favorite of my daughter, who always preferred it to catsup. Here we have added some flavorings and brushed it over baked fish slices. Shark is a dark, firm-fleshed fish that should be soaked in skim milk 30 minutes and drained before using.

6 Servings

Shark

1¼–1½ lbs. shark steaks, cut into 6 serving-size pieces

1 cup skim milk, for soaking fish

Hoisin Sauce

2 cloves garlic, minced

½ teaspoon fresh ginger root, grated

6 tablespoons Hoisin sauce, found in most large supermarkets and oriental food stores

1 teaspoon light soy sauce

½ teaspoon sesame oil

2 tablespoons dry white wine

½ cup chives, minced

Shark: Wash fish and cut into serving-size pieces. Place in shallow bowl and cover with milk. Let stand 30 minutes. Drain.

Hoisin Sauce: In small bowl, mix garlic, ginger, Hoisin sauce, soy sauce, sesame oil, and wine.

If seaweed is available, spread it over a cookie sheet. Place shark on seaweed. Preheat oven to 400° F. Brush shark with Hoisin Sauce. Bake fish until done, 10 to 12 minutes. Fish will be slightly firm to the touch when done and flesh will darken slightly. To serve, sprinkle with chives.

Nutritional Data

PER SERVING		EXCHANGES	
Calories:	137	Milk:	0.0
Fat (gm):	3.9	Veg.:	1.0
Sat. fat (gm):	0.8	Fruit:	0.0
Cholesterol (mg):	39	Bread:	0.0
Sodium (mg):	290	Meat:	2.0
% Calories from fat:	26	Fat:	0.0

GROUPER EN PAPILLOTE WITH MUSHROOMS

This fish, a member of the bass family, is found along the Atlantic coast.

6 Servings

Ginger Marinade
- ½ cup cider vinegar
- ½ teaspoon fresh ginger root, grated

Grouper

1¼–1½ lbs. grouper fillets, cut into 6 servings

Vegetables
- 1 tablespoon canola oil, or non-stick cooking spray
- 3 cloves garlic
- 3 green onions, minced
- 2 teaspoons chervil
- 2 cups brown mushrooms, sliced
- 6 brown mushrooms, trimmed, left whole for garnish
- Parchment paper

Ginger Marinade: Combine vinegar and ginger in bowl.

Grouper: Put fish in large self-sealing plastic bag and pour in marinade. Seal bag securely and turn it several times so that all surfaces of fish are touched by marinade. Place bag in shallow dish and marinate in refrigerator 1 hour. Drain.

Vegetables: Prepare while fish is marinating. Spray a frying pan and saute garlic, onions, and chervil until onions are soft, 4 to 5 minutes, stirring occasionally. Add 2 cups mushrooms and continue cooking until mushrooms are tender and dry. Set aside.

Again spray a frying pan and saute remaining 6 mushrooms until browned and cooked. Reserve for garnish; reheat just before serving.

Cut 6 pieces of parchment paper into heart-shaped designs, each large enough to hold one piece of fish. Position fish on paper. Spoon about ¼ cup of the mushroom mixture onto each fish serving.

Fold the paper to encase the fish servings. Turn the paper in at the top to close each papillote.

Using spatula, set fish on baking sheet. Preheat oven to 400° F. and bake fish 10–12 minutes, depending on thickness. Remove one papillote from oven to see if fish is done (opaque and flakes easily). If not, continue cooking until done to taste. Remove fish packets from oven and place directly on dinner plates for guests to open. Garnish each plate with one large brown mushroom. Serve hot.

Nutritional Data

PER SERVING		EXCHANGES	
Calories:	116	Milk:	0.0
Fat (gm):	3.3	Veg.:	0.0
Sat. fat (gm):	0.4	Fruit:	0.0
Cholesterol (mg):	35	Bread:	0.0
Sodium (mg):	40	Meat:	2.0
% Calories from fat:	26	Fat:	0.0

GROUPER WITH BANANAS

The grouper is wrapped in aluminum foil and baked to perfection. The addition of bananas gives this recipe a special tropical taste and dimension.

6 Servings

1¼–1½ lbs. grouper, cut into serving-size portions
1 teaspoon honey mustard
    Olive oil, or non-stick cooking spray
    Aluminum foil
2 tablespoons orange juice, freshly squeezed
1 teaspoon thyme
½ teaspoon ground cinnamon
3 bananas, peeled, cut vertically

L ightly brush fish with mustard. Spray 6 pieces of foil, each large enough to hold one fish serving. Place fish pieces on the foil.

Mix together orange juice, thyme, and cinnamon. Sprinkle mixture over fish. Place 1 banana half over each piece of fish. Fold foil to seal fish packets.

Preheat oven to 400° F. Put packets in glass baking dish, and bake 10 to 12 minutes or until fish is cooked. To test doneness, remove one packet, open it, and check to see if fish is opaque.

Set an individual packet on each plate, allowing guests to open the packets themselves. (You can also wrap the fish in lettuce or spinach instead of aluminum foil before baking.

Nutritional Data

PER SERVING		EXCHANGES	
Calories:	142	Milk:	0.0
Fat (gm):	1.3	Veg.:	0.0
Sat. fat (gm):	0.3	Fruit:	1.0
Cholesterol (mg):	34	Bread:	0.0
Sodium (mg):	51	Meat:	2.0
% Calories from fat:	8	Fat:	0.0

GROUPER BAKED IN ROMAINE LEAVES

Grouper is a firm, coarse fish, which can be used as steaks or fillets.

6 Servings

Green Bell Pepper Sauce

- 3 green bell peppers
- ½ cup dry white wine
- ½ teaspoon chervil
- ¼ teaspoon white pepper
- 2 tablespoons non-fat plain yogurt

Grouper

- 12 Romaine, or Boston, lettuce leaves, trimmed
- 1¼–1½ lbs. grouper fillets, cut into 6 serving pieces
- ½ teaspoon red pepper flakes
- 3 tablespoons lime juice, freshly squeezed
- ½ cup julienne carrots
- ½ cup julienne celery
- ½ cup julienne fennel

Green Bell Pepper Sauce: Heat peppers under broiler about 3 minutes, turning once or twice. Peppers will be charred on all sides. Quickly put peppers in plastic bag and seal. Let stand 5 minutes. Remove peppers and discard skins, which will peel off easily. Cut peppers into pieces and put in saucepan. Add wine, chervil, and pepper. Simmer 3 minutes. Let cool and then puree. Serve sauce over the fish bundles, adding the yogurt at the last minute.

Grouper: Blanch the lettuce leaves in simmering water 45 seconds. Drain. Place each fish serving on 2 leaves. Sprinkle with red pepper and lime juice.

Cook vegetables in simmering water until almost tender. Drain. Arrange vegetables evenly over fish. Wrap fish in lettuce, envelope style, making 6 fish bundles.

Preheat oven to 400° F. Place fish bundles on sprayed cookie sheet. Cover bundles with aluminum foil lightly during baking. Bake 12 to 15 minutes, depending on thickness of fish. Spoon Green Pepper Sauce over bundles at the table.

Nutritional Data

PER SERVING		EXCHANGES	
Calories:	132	Milk:	0.0
Fat (gm):	1.2	Veg.:	1.0
Sat. fat (gm):	0.2	Fruit:	0.0
Cholesterol (mg):	35	Bread:	0.0
Sodium (mg):	109	Meat:	2.0
% Calories from fat:	8	Fat:	0.0

STEAMED GROUPER WITH TURNIPS

Dr. Lolly Levit told me about fragrant turnips. Her cousin in Germany had given her the recipe. It is a sweet and tangy flavoring for grouper, which is a mild, rather delicate fish that lends itself to steaming.

6 Servings

            3 cups turnips, thinly sliced
               Olive oil, or non-stick cooking spray
            3 large shallots, minced
            3 tablespoons sugar
            2 tablespoons red wine vinegar
    1¼–1½ lbs. grouper fillets, cut into 6 servings
            2 oranges, sliced thin
            2 tablespoons orange rind, grated
            ¼ cup parsley, minced

Cut turnips into matchstick pieces and par-boil. Drain and set aside.

Spray a frying pan and saute shallots until soft, stirring occasionally. Sprinkle shallots with sugar and continue cooking until sugar turns golden brown, stirring almost constantly so as not to let sugar burn. Stir in vinegar and turnips. Partially cover and cook over medium heat until turnips are tender. Set aside.

Meanwhile place the grouper on orange slices set on a steaming rack (or an inverted dish over water). Bring water to a boil, then reduce heat to simmer. Cover steamer with tight-fitting lid. Steam 5–8 minutes or until done. Fish will be opaque and slightly firm to the touch. Cool 4 to 5 minutes.

Using a spatula, transfer fish to individual dishes. Spread turnips around the fish. Sprinkle fish with orange rind and parsley. Serve hot.

Nutritional Data

PER SERVING		EXCHANGES	
Calories:	146	Milk:	0.0
Fat (gm):	1.1	Veg.:	1.0
Sat. fat (gm):	0.2	Fruit:	0.0
Cholesterol (mg):	35	Bread:	0.0
Sodium (mg):	80	Meat:	2.0
% Calories from fat:	6	Fat:	0.0

Sweet-and-Sour Grouper

You can serve this dish hot or cold. Try it both ways and see which style you like best. The general rule of thumb governing pepper is that white pepper is used in dishes with white food, that is fish, chicken, and eggs, and black pepper is used in dishes that are dark, such as meat.

4 Servings

Olive oil, or non-stick cooking spray
1¼–1½ lbs. grouper, cut into serving-size portions
1 cup onions, sliced
⅓ cup red wine vinegar
1½ teaspoons each: minced parsley; sugar
1 teaspoon basil
½ teaspoon mint, chopped
¼ teaspoon white pepper

S pray a skillet and pan fry grouper until just done. Turn once, using spatula. Fish will be opaque and flake easily when prodded with fork. Remove fish and set aside.

Spray pan again and fry onions until tender, 4 to 5 minutes, over medium heat, stirring occasionally. Stir in vinegar, parsley, sugar, basil, mint, and white pepper. Cover pan and simmer 4 to 5 minutes.

Place fish in sauce and cover. Again, simmer 2 minutes or until fish is hot. Place fish in individual dishes and serve with pasta salad.

If serving fish cold, put fish in shallow bowl and drizzle sauce over it. Cover and refrigerate overnight.

Nutritional Data

PER SERVING		EXCHANGES	
Calories:	153	Milk:	0.0
Fat (gm):	1.5	Veg.:	0.0
Sat. fat (gm):	0.3	Fruit:	0.0
Cholesterol (mg):	52	Bread:	0.0
Sodium (mg):	60	Meat:	3.0
% Calories from fat:	9	Fat:	0.0

FINNAN HADDIE

Finnan haddie is an English expression for smoked haddock. The haddock is smoked to a golden color and smoky flavor. It is available in larger fish markets.

6 Servings

1¼–1½ lbs. finnan haddie (smoked haddock),
     defrosted if necessary
2 cups skimmed milk
1 teaspoon cholesterol-free margarine
2 cups white mushrooms, sliced
1 onion, sliced thin
1 teaspoon stone-ground mustard
3 hard-cooked egg whites, chopped
¼ cup chives, chopped

C over fish with water and let stand in bowl 1 hour. Drain. Cut fish in quarters and put in saucepan. Cover finnan haddie with milk. Simmer 15 to 20 minutes, covered. Drain and flake fish. Discard milk.

Heat margarine in non-stick frying pan. Saute onion and mushrooms until tender, about 5 minutes, over medium heat, stirring occasionally. Stir in mustard and flaked fish.

Spoon fish onto individual dishes, sprinkle with egg whites and chives, and serve hot. You might want to serve finnan haddie with toast points or cooked white rice.

Nutritional Data

PER SERVING		EXCHANGES	
Calories:	138	Milk:	0.0
Fat (gm):	1.4	Veg.:	0.0
Sat. fat (gm):	0.2	Fruit:	0.0
Cholesterol (mg):	72	Bread:	0.0
Sodium (mg):	758	Meat:	3.0
% Calories from fat:	9	Fat:	0.0

FISH CHOP SUEY

Chop suey is just a fish and vegetable stir-fry. Serve with cooked white rice or whole-wheat noodles and watch it just disappear.

6 Servings

Canola oil, or non-stick cooking spray
3 cloves garlic, minced
½ teaspoon fresh ginger root, grated
2 onions, sliced
1½ cups bok-choy, shredded
1½ cups celery, sliced
1 lb. grouper fillets, cut into ½-in. pieces
1 can (6½ ozs.) water chestnuts, drained, sliced
½ cup water
2 tablespoons light soy sauce
½ teaspoon brown sugar
1 tablespoon cornstarch

H eat wok or non-stick frying pan sprayed with oil. Stir-fry garlic, ginger, and onions over high heat. Add bok-choy and celery, and stir-fry about 2 minutes. Add fish pieces and water chestnuts. Stir-fry about another 2 minutes or until done. Fish will be opaque.

Quickly mix together water, soy sauce, sugar, and cornstarch. Stir it into the chop suey mixture, trying not to break up fish pieces. Sauce will cook in 1 to 2 minutes and thicken slightly.

Serve chop suey hot, with or without rice.

Nutritional Data

PER SERVING		EXCHANGES	
Calories:	180	Milk:	0.0
Fat (gm):	1.2	Veg.:	3.0
Sat. fat (gm):	0.3	Fruit:	0.0
Cholesterol (mg):	28	Bread:	0.0
Sodium (mg):	251	Meat:	2.0
% Calories from fat:	6	Fat:	0.0

SEAFOOD BARBECUED PIZZA

There are many good brands of ready-to-serve pizza crusts available on supermarket shelves. But we will make our own crust for this recipe. It can be prepared a day before, rolled out, covered, and refrigerated until ready to bake.

12 Servings

Cornmeal Crust
- 1 package dry yeast
- 1 cup warm water
- 1 tablespoon olive oil, optional
- 1¾ cups all-purpose flour
- 1 cup yellow cornmeal
- Olive oil, or non-stick cooking spray

Seafood Barbecue Sauce
- 1 can (16 ozs.) chopped tomatoes, pureed, include liquid
- 2 teaspoons oregano
- ¾ teaspoon fennel seeds
- 1 teaspoon each: chili powder; cumin
- ½ teaspoon garlic powder
- ¾ lb. canned tuna
- 2 cups red bell peppers, thinly sliced

Cornmeal Crust: Dissolve yeast in warm water. Combine olive oil with flour and cornmeal. Mix in the yeast. It is easy and convenient to prepare crust in a food processor fitted with steel blade. It will make a soft dough.

Turn the dough out onto a lightly floured board and knead until smooth. Place dough in ungreased bowl, cover lightly, and let rise until double in bulk, about 1 hour.

Punch dough down and press with heel of your hand or use small rolling pin to spread dough onto a 9 × 12-inch cookie sheet or pizza pan that has been sprayed with oil. Set aside.

Seafood Barbecue Sauce: Combine tomatoes, oregano, fennel, chili powder, cumin, and garlic powder in small saucepan. Bring sauce to a boil over medium heat. Reduce heat to simmer and continue cooking 5 minutes, stirring occasionally. Cool.

Brush pizza crust with 1 cup of sauce. Break up fish into flakes or small pieces and sprinkle it and peppers over crust.

Preheat oven to 425° F. Set pizza on pizza tile and bake 20 minutes or until done to taste. Pizza is done when crust is golden brown and topping is hot. Serve immediately.

Nutritional Data

PER SERVING		EXCHANGES	
Calories:	140	Milk:	0.0
Fat (gm):	0.9	Veg.:	1.0
Sat. fat (gm):	0.1	Fruit:	0.0
Cholesterol (mg):	10	Bread:	1.0
Sodium (mg):	119	Meat:	1.0
% Calories from fat:	6	Fat:	0.0

6.
SHELLFISH

Mussels
Clams
Crab
Scallops
Shrimp
Lobster

MUSSEL BUNDLES

For a beautiful, dramatic presentation, why not grill the mussels on a bed of seaweed instead of packaging them in aluminum foil. Seaweed is sometimes available at the local fish market; check and see. Ask your fishmonger to check over the mussels and give you only the best ones.

4 Servings (appetizer-size)

Double-strength aluminum foil
16 mussels, washed; remove beards and discard any open mussels
8 tablespoons dry white wine
½ cup onions, chopped
4 cloves garlic, minced
½ cup parsley, minced
½ teaspoon each: basil; tarragon; thyme

C ut aluminum foil to hold 4 mussels per sheet. Divide mussels and set 4 in the center of each piece of foil. Sprinkle wine, onions, garlic, parsley, and herbs over mussels. Bring up sides of foil to make bundles.

To grill mussel packages, place them directly on grill over hot coals. Cook 3 to 4 minutes. Turn packages over and grill another 2 minutes. Remove one package from grill and carefully open it to see if mussels have opened. If not, return it to grill and continue cooking until mussels are done.

Place one bundle of mussels on each of 4 plates. Direct guests to discard any unopened mussels. Serve with crusty bread.

Nutritional Data

PER SERVING		EXCHANGES	
Calories:	41	Milk:	0.0
Fat (gm):	0.4	Veg.:	0.0
Sat. fat (gm):	0.0	Fruit:	0.0
Cholesterol (mg):	8	Bread:	0.0
Sodium (mg):	46	Meat:	1.0
% Calories from fat:	8	Fat:	0.0

GRILLED MUSSELS WITH RELISH

Nowadays, most mussels are farm raised and therefore require only washing. If the mussels are from the ocean, they will have a brownish "beard," which must be removed by using a small sharp knife. Discard any open mussels before grilling, and discard any closed mussels after grilling.

4 Servings

Tomato Relish

- 2 large tomatoes, peeled, seeded, chopped
- ½ cup chili sauce
- 2 green onions, minced
- 1 cup cucumber, seeded, chopped
- ½ teaspoon each: balsamic vinegar; celery seed
- ¼ teaspoon each: oregano; salt; pepper

Mussels

3–3½ dozen mussels, washed; remove beards and discard any open mussels.

Tomato Relish: Mix together tomatoes, chili sauce, green onions, cucumber, vinegar, celery seed, oregano, salt, and pepper. Cover lightly and refrigerate until needed. Stir before serving.

Mussels: Place on grill rack over hot coals. Cover grill and cook 3 to 6 minutes or until mussels pop open. Discard any unopened mussels.

Transfer mussels to individual bowls. Drizzle Tomato Relish over mussels and serve hot. Provide an extra bowl for discarded shells. Serve with crusty French bread.

Nutritional Data

PER SERVING		EXCHANGES	
Calories:	103	Milk:	0.0
Fat (gm):	1.5	Veg.:	1.0
Sat. fat (gm):	0.0	Fruit:	0.0
Cholesterol (mg):	32	Bread:	0.0
Sodium (mg):	704	Meat:	1.5
% Calories from fat:	13	Fat:	0.0

MICROWAVE THAI MUSSELS

Microwave mussels on their sides, the larger side down, and in a single layer. Wash mussels well and discard any that are open before cooking; discard any mussels that are closed after cooking.

2 Servings

Thai Flavoring

    Olive oil, or non-stick cooking oil

3 cloves garlic, minced

½ cup breadcrumbs

¼ teaspoon pepper

1 teaspoon Thailand commercially bottled fish sauce

⅓ cup cilantro, minced

Mussels

16 mussels, well scrubbed

Thai Flavorings: Spray non-stick frying pan and saute garlic 1 minute, or until cooked, stirring occasionally, over medium heat. Add breadcrumbs, pepper, fish sauce, and minced cilantro. Cook over low heat until crumbs are just toasted. Remove from heat and reserve.

Mussels: Using a microwave-safe glass dish, pie plate or deep dish, arrange mussels on sides, keeping them in a single layer. Cover dish securely with plastic wrap for the microwave. Microwave 1½ to 2 minutes or until mussels are open.

Remove dish from microwave and take off plastic wrap, allowing steam to escape away from you. Remove mussels, with liquid, to a deep dish. Sprinkle with Thai Flavoring.

Nutritional Data

PER SERVING		EXCHANGES	
Calories:	254	Milk:	0.0
Fat (gm):	4.7	Veg.:	0.0
Sat. fat (gm):	0.3	Fruit:	0.0
Cholesterol (mg):	85	Bread:	1.0
Sodium (mg):	651	Meat:	3.0
% Calories from fat:	17	Fat:	0.0

STEAMED CLAMS OVER SPAGHETTI

How lucky for those of us who are looking for low-cholesterol products to discover low-cholesterol spaghetti. It's available at large supermarkets nationwide.

4 Servings

24 fresh clams, scrubbed; remember, if clams are open before cooking, do not use them; if they are not open after cooking, discard them.
   Non-stick cooking spray
4 cloves garlic, minced
1 cup onions, minced
¼ cup parsley, minced
½ teaspoon oregano
¼ teaspoon white pepper
1 cup water
3 cups hot, cooked spaghetti
4 teaspoons Parmesan cheese, freshly grated

Scrub clams and rinse well under cold running water.
Spray a frying pan, and saute garlic and onions for about 4 minutes, stirring occasionally, over medium heat. Add parsley, oregano, and white pepper. Add clams and water. Cover tightly; steam over medium heat 5 minutes or until clams open. Discard any unopened clams.
Spoon spaghetti into soup bowls. Arrange clams over spaghetti; pour broth into bowls. Sprinkle with Parmesan cheese, and serve hot.

Nutritional Data

PER SERVING		EXCHANGES	
Calories:	296	Milk:	0.0
Fat (gm):	3.1	Veg.:	0.0
Sat. fat (gm):	0.6	Fruit:	0.0
Cholesterol (mg):	57	Bread:	2.0
Sodium (mg):	136	Meat:	3.0
% Calories from fat:	10	Fat:	0.0

CLAM DIP

Although this recipe is for an appetizer, we chose to include it because it also doubles as a cold dressing for fish.

6 Servings

1 cup low-fat, small-curd cottage cheese
3 cloves garlic
1 can (8 ozs.) clams, drained, minced
½ teaspoon each: tarragon; garlic powder
¼ teaspoon pepper
1 cup green or red bell pepper strips
1 cup snow peas, trimmed
1 cup cucumber slices

U sing food processor fitted with steel blade, or a blender, puree cheese and garlic. Add clams, tarragon, garlic powder, and pepper. Mix well. Pour into bowl, cover, and refrigerate until serving time.

When ready to serve, mix dip and taste to adjust seasonings. Put bowl in center of large plate. Surround bowl with cut vegetables and serve.

Nutritional Data

PER SERVING		EXCHANGES	
Calories:	92	Milk:	0.0
Fat (gm):	1.1	Veg.:	0.5
Sat. fat (gm):	0.3	Fruit:	0.0
Cholesterol (mg):	24	Bread:	0.0
Sodium (mg):	192	Meat:	1.5
% Calories from fat:	11	Fat:	0.0

CLAM DIP PITA PIZZAS

What could be easier than making a pizza and not having to prepare the crust. We used whole-wheat pita bread; split one open, and you have an instant crust.

6 Servings

3 whole-wheat pita breads
2 cups clam dip (see preceding recipe)
½ teaspoon each: sage; rosemary
1 cup green onions, chopped

P ry apart each pita and lay each half flat. Spread bread with clam dip. Sprinkle with sage, rosemary, and green onions.

Using a spatula, put pita pizzas on cookie sheet. Preheat oven to 425° F. Bake 7 to 10 minutes or until breads are just crisp. Remove to serving plate and serve hot.

Nutritional Data

PER SERVING		EXCHANGES	
Calories:	148	Milk:	0.0
Fat (gm):	1.4	Veg.:	0.0
Sat. fat (gm):	0.3	Fruit:	0.0
Cholesterol (mg):	24	Bread:	1.0
Sodium (mg):	300	Meat:	1.5
% Calories from fat:	9	Fat:	0.0

CRABMEAT FU YONG

We use only 1 egg yolk in the preparation of Crab Fu Yong. It is the addition of egg whites instead of whole eggs that makes this dish "skinny" and good to enjoy. This recipe may also be made with mussels or shrimp instead of crab.

4 Servings

- 1 egg
- 4 egg whites
- 2 teaspoons cornstarch
- 4 ozs. fresh or defrosted crabmeat, drained, shredded
- 4 reconstituted oriental mushrooms, stems discarded, shredded
- 2 green onions, minced
- ⅛ teaspoon each: white pepper; garlic powder
- 1 tablespoon dry white wine
   Canola oil, or non-stick cooking spray

Lightly beat egg and egg whites. Mix cornstarch and crabmeat with eggs. Add mushrooms, onions, pepper, garlic powder, and wine.

Spray a non-stick frying pan with oil. Ladle crab-egg mixture into pan, making pancakes. Cook over medium heat. Turn once. Pancakes are done when egg is firm and slightly brown around the edges. Continue cooking until all pancakes are done. Good as lunch, a first course, or a light dinner.

Nutritional Data

PER SERVING		EXCHANGES	
Calories:	83	Milk:	0.0
Fat (gm):	1.8	Veg.:	1.0
Sat. fat (gm):	0.5	Fruit:	0.0
Cholesterol (mg):	80	Bread:	0.0
Sodium (mg):	146	Meat:	1.0
% Calories from fat:	20	Fat:	0.0

CRAB LEGS WITH MIDDLE-EASTERN VEGETABLES

King crab legs are available frozen and precooked. Defrost the legs in your refrigerator. They can be steamed or grilled.

4 Servings

2 lbs. frozen, split king crab legs, presliced in half, defrosted in refrigerator

1 small eggplant, cut into ½-in. pieces, sprinkled with salt, drained 30 minutes; wash, pat dry

2 red bell peppers, seeded, quartered lengthwise

1 red onion, sliced

1 medium zucchini, trimmed, cut into ½-in. slices

Brushing Sauce

½ cup red wine vinegar

2 tablespoons dark brown sugar

½ teaspoon oregano

¼ teaspoon pepper

2 tablespoons capers, for garnish

P lace crab legs in steamer over water that has been brought to a boil and reduced to medium heat. Cover tightly and steam only until crab legs are heated, 5 to 10 minutes. Remove one leg to see if it is hot.

If you prefer to grill the crab legs at the same time you are grilling the vegetables, arrange 3 pieces of soaked (30 minutes) and drained wood (apple wood or mesquite) over hot coals. Place crab legs, cut side down, on hot grill. Cover and cook 4 minutes or until legs are hot and browned slightly.

Brushing Sauce: Combine ingredients and brush vegetables lightly. Set them on grill rack over hot coals. Cook vegetables 4 to 5 minutes, turning as necessary until done: vegetables will be tender and char slightly. Remove vegetables to a platter and arrange decoratively. Serve with crab legs and garnish with capers.

Nutritional Data

PER SERVING		EXCHANGES	
Calories:	117	Milk:	0.0
Fat (gm):	1.1	Veg.:	1.0
Sat. fat (gm):	0.1	Fruit:	0.0
Cholesterol (mg):	30	Bread:	0.0
Sodium (mg):	613	Meat:	1.5
% Calories from fat:	8	Fat:	0.0

Soft-Shelled Crabs with Herb Breading

Soft-shelled crabs are blue crabs that have shed their shells and begun to harden new shells. From the middle of April to September these tender, completely edible crabs are available. Ask your fishmonger to clean them for you. If you do it yourself, cut off the face and discard the tails. Lift the side spine and discard the gills (feathery) that are inside the crab. I find it easier to have crabs cleaned for me rather than tackle this difficult task. Soft-shelled crabs are found from Delaware Bay to Florida.

4 Servings

Olive oil, or non-stick cooking spray
2 teaspoons no-cholesterol margarine
4 cloves garlic, minced
¼ cup shallots, minced
¼ cup Italian-flavored breadcrumbs
8 soft-shelled crabs, cleaned, washed, patted dry
¼ teaspoon each: pepper; chervil; thyme
¼ cup chives, minced

Prepare crabs and set aside.

Spray a non-stick frying pan and add margarine. Saute garlic and shallots until just beginning to brown, over medium heat, stirring occasionally. Mix in breadcrumbs. Add crabs and saute over medium heat, turning once until cooked. Crabs will brown when cooked. Sprinkle crabs with pepper and chervil.

Place 2 crabs on each plate. Sprinkle with crumbs and chives. Serve hot. You might want to serve one crab as an appetizer course.

Nutritional Data

PER SERVING		EXCHANGES	
Calories:	100	Milk:	0.0
Fat (gm):	2.2	Veg.:	1.0
Sat. fat (gm):	0.4	Fruit:	0.0
Cholesterol (mg):	54	Bread:	0.0
Sodium (mg):	220	Meat:	1.5
% Calories from fat:	21	Fat:	0.0

Marinated Scallop Burritos

Scallops come in beautiful shells that are "scalloped" in texture and design. This mollusk comes in two sizes. The small bay scallop is from Atlantic shores. It is tender and delicate tasting. The deep-sea scallop is larger and somewhat tougher in taste.

6 Servings

Hot Tomato Salsa

- 3 large tomatoes, peeled, seeded, chopped
- 3 jalapeño peppers, seeded, chopped (use rubber gloves and do not touch eyes after touching peppers)
- 3 cloves garlic, minced
- ½ cup cilantro, minced
- ¼ teaspoon pepper

Scallops

- 24 scallops, wash and pat dry

Marinade

- ¼ cup tarragon vinegar
- 2 tablespoons olive oil
- 2 tablespoons cilantro
- ½ teaspoon each: cumin powder; chili powder

Accompaniments

- 6 small flour tortillas
- 1 red bell pepper, seeded, chopped, for garnish

Hot Tomato Salsa: Chop tomatoes and put them in small glass bowl. Mix in peppers, garlic, cilantro, and pepper. Cover lightly and refrigerate until serving time.

Scallops: Bring about 1 quart of water to a boil over medium high heat. Add scallops and simmer 3 to 4 minutes or until scallops turn opaque. Drain well; pat dry. Transfer to plastic bag.

Marinade: Combine ingredients and pour into plastic bag with scallops. Seal securely and turn bag several times so that marinade touches all surfaces of the scallops. Place in shallow dish and refrigerate overnight.

At serving time, separate marinade and scallops. Show your guests how to assemble a burrito: put 4 scallops on a warm tortilla, spoon Tomato Salsa over scallops, and sprinkle with peppers. Roll up tortilla, making a burrito. Fold in one end and begin eating at the open end. You might want to serve refried black beans and rice and/or a salad.

Nutritional Data

PER SERVING		EXCHANGES	
Calories:	150	Milk:	0.0
Fat (gm):	3.3	Veg.:	0.5
Sat. fat (gm):	0.3	Fruit:	0.0
Cholesterol (mg):	19	Bread:	0.5
Sodium (mg):	213	Meat:	2.0
% Calories from fat:	20	Fat:	0.0

SCALLOP STIR-FRY

You could substitute lobster, cut in pieces, or in or out of the shell shrimp.

6 Servings

- 2 teaspoons cornstarch
- ½ teaspoon sugar
- ¼ teaspoon salt
- 1 teaspoon light soy sauce
- ½ cup chicken stock
  Canola oil, or non-stick cooking spray
- 3 cloves garlic, minced
- ¾ lb. scallops
- ½ cup reconstituted shiitake mushrooms
- ½ lb. snow peas, trimmed
- 1 cup water chestnuts, sliced
- 12 cashews

Mix cornstarch with sugar, salt, soy sauce, and stock; set aside.
Spray a wok or frying pan with oil. Saute garlic until
cooked. Add scallops and mushrooms; stir-fry 30 seconds. Add snow peas
and water chestnuts; stir fry another 30 seconds. Stir in cornstarch mixture. Simmer, stirring constantly, until sauce thickens slightly, 1 to 2
minutes, and scallops are just cooked.
Spoon food into small bowls and top each bowl with 2 nuts. Serve
with green, brown, or white rice.

Nutritional Data

PER SERVING		EXCHANGES	
Calories:	127	Milk:	0.0
Fat (gm):	2.9	Veg.:	2.0
Sat. fat (gm):	0.5	Fruit:	0.0
Cholesterol (mg):	19	Bread:	0.0
Sodium (mg):	282	Meat:	1.5
% Calories from fat:	20	Fat:	0.0

Down-Under Shrimp with Kiwi

If fresh dill is not available, substitute half of the amount with dried dill. Instead of soaking the shrimp in a marinade, we brush a small amount of marinade over them.

5 Servings

Lemon Marinade
- 1 teaspoon extra virgin olive oil
- 2 teaspoons lemon juice, freshly squeezed
- 1 teaspoon fresh dill, chopped
- ½ teaspoon red pepper, crushed

Shrimp
- 1¼ lbs. large or jumbo shrimp, peeled, deveined

Cucumber Sauce
- 2 cups plain non-fat yogurt
- 1 cup cucumbers, seeded, chopped
- 1 teaspoon dill, chopped
- ¼ teaspoon pepper

- 4 kiwis, peeled, cut in halves
- Canola oil, or non-stick cooking spray
- 4 short double-pronged skewers

Lemon Marinade: Combine all marinade ingredients.

Shrimp: Brush lightly with marinade. Let shrimp stand 30 minutes.

Cucumber Sauce: Mix together yogurt, cucumber, dill, and pepper. Cover lightly and refrigerate until needed.

Thread half a kiwi on skewer, add shrimp, and end with remaining half of kiwi. Set skewers on sprayed grill or grill rack over hot coals. Grill shrimp 2 to 3 minutes on each side or until they are no longer translucent.

Transfer shrimp and kiwi to individual dishes. Pass Cucumber Sauce at the table.

Nutritional Data

PER SERVING		EXCHANGES	
Calories:	188	Milk:	0.5
Fat (gm):	2.3	Veg.:	0.0
Sat. fat (gm):	0.5	Fruit:	0.5
Cholesterol (mg):	176	Bread:	0.0
Sodium (mg):	379	Meat:	2.0
% Calories from fat:	11	Fat:	0.0

SHRIMP PIZZA ON THE GRILL

This is an easy summer pizza: simply grill the shrimp and top a pizza with it. You might even ask your guests to help you put the finishing touches on the pizza.

12 Servings

Cornmeal Crust

- 1 package dry yeast
- 1 cup warm water
- 1 tablespoon olive oil, optional
- 1¾ cups all-purpose flour
- 1 cup yellow cornmeal

Topping

- ¾ cup sun-dried tomatoes, cut into slivers, soaked in water, drained
- 3 cups low-fat, skim-milk cottage cheese
- 4 cloves garlic, minced
- 3 tablespoons skim milk
- 1 tablespoon basil
- 1 lb. small shrimp, peeled, deveined, washed, patted dry

Cornmeal Crust: Dissolve yeast in water. Combine olive oil with flour and cornmeal. Mix in yeast. It is easy and convenient to prepare crust in a food processor fitted with steel blade. It will make a soft dough.

Turn dough out onto lightly floured board and knead until smooth. Place dough in ungreased bowl, cover lightly, and let rise until double in bulk, about 1 hour. Punch dough down and press with heel of your hand, or use small rolling pin. Divide dough in half, and roll both halves out to rectangular or circle shapes.

Topping: Sliver tomatoes, soaked until soft in hot water, and drain. Set aside. Prepare cheese topping using a food processor or blender. Puree the cheese. Add garlic, milk, and basil. Spread cheese over pizza crusts. Sprinkle pizzas with tomatoes and shrimp.

Prepare grill. When coals are hot and pizza tile is preheated, begin grilling pizzas. Place pizzas on grill, using a paddle. Cover grill and cook 5 to 10 minutes or until pizza is cooked. Crust will be golden brown and topping hot.

Remove pizzas, using paddle and long-handled spatula. Cut into pieces and serve hot.

Nutritional Data

PER SERVING		EXCHANGES	
Calories:	184	Milk:	0.0
Fat (gm):	1.5	Veg.:	0.0
Sat. fat (gm):	0.5	Fruit:	0.0
Cholesterol (mg):	60	Bread:	1.0
Sodium (mg):	305	Meat:	2.0
% Calories from fat:	7	Fat:	0.0

STEAMED MAINE LOBSTER WITH SHRIMP SAUCE

Steamed lobster is probably the easiest recipe for the most flair in the seafood category. Try it and see if you don't agree. Cut lobster in half with a cleaver or large, sharp knife before serving.

Some rules of thumb for eating a whole lobster:

1. Twist off claws. Using a nutcracker or lobster cracker, break open the claws. With a small fork or pick, remove the lobster meat.

2. Remove meat from the tail using a small fork or pick. Break off the small side legs and open with your hands. You can suck out the lobster meat.

3. Remove the black vein that runs down the body of the lobster. Also discard the sac at the base of the head. Some lobsters contain coral-colored roe, which is delicious. Serve napkins, nutcrackers, lobster picks, or small forks, and lots of napkins.

4 Servings

Shrimp Sauce

- ¼ cup shallots, chopped
- ½ cup cooked shrimp, chopped
  Canola oil, or non-stick cooking spray
- 1 tablespoon margarine
- 1 tablespoon all-purpose flour
- ½ cup fish stock
- 2 tablespoons skimmed or 2% milk
- ¼ teaspoon ground cardamom

Lobster

- 2 whole lobsters, 1-1/4–1-1/2 lbs.
  Seaweed or lime wedges for garnish

Shrimp Sauce: Saute shallots in sprayed small saucepan until soft. Stir in shrimp and cook 1 minute. Set aside.

In another small saucepan, melt margarine. Whisk in flour and continue cooking and stirring until flour is absorbed. Add fish stock, milk, cardamom, and shrimp. Stir until sauce thickens slightly. Serve hot.

Lobster: Heat water to a boil in steamer or kettle. If using a rack on a pan, the pan must rise at least 1 inch above water level. Put lobsters on rack and cover pot. Reduce heat to simmer and steam lobsters 12 to 15 minutes; the rule of thumb is 10 minutes per pound.

Carefully remove lobsters and cut in half for four servings. Pass Shrimp Sauce at the table. Lobsters are sweet and moist, and although they are classically served with drawn butter, we find that this recipe, without it, works just great.

Nutritional Data

PER SERVING		EXCHANGES	
Calories:	128	Milk:	0.0
Fat (gm):	2.2	Veg.:	0.0
Sat. fat (gm):	0.4	Fruit:	0.0
Cholesterol (mg):	95	Bread:	0.0
Sodium (mg):	443	Meat:	2.5
% Calories from fat:	16	Fat:	0.0

7.
GRILLED AND SMOKED RECIPES

Catfish

Orange Roughy

Red Snapper

Haddock

Whitefish

Clams

Scallops

Shrimp

Lobster

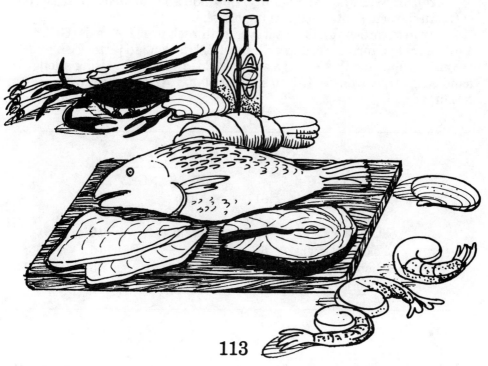

CAJUN CATFISH ON THE GRILL

For the most part, catfish is now farm raised. So it is readily available and consistent in flavor. It makes an excellent choice for Cajun preparation, which has become classic American.

4 Servings

Cajun Spice Rub
(makes about ⅓ cup)

- 4 teaspoons paprika
- 1 tablespoon cayenne
- 2 teaspoons garlic powder
- 1 teaspoon each: oregano; onion powder
- ½ cup whole-wheat breadcrumbs

Catfish
- 1¼ lbs. catfish fillets, or 4 servings
- Canola oil, or non-stick cooking spray

Cajun Spice Rub: To make the Cajun Rub, mix together paprika, cayenne, garlic powder, oregano, onion powder, and breadcrumbs. Let spices stand 30 minutes to allow flavors to meld together.

Catfish: Wash fish and pat dry. Sprinkle and rub about ½ teaspoon of Cajun flavoring onto each serving of fish.

Arrange catfish fillets on sprayed grill rack over hot coals. Grill fish 4 to 5 minutes, turn once, and grill until fish is done to taste. Fish will become opaque and flake easily when prodded with fork. Using a long-handled spatula, transfer fish to serving platter. Good served with cornbread.

Nutritional Data

PER SERVING		EXCHANGES	
Calories:	181	Milk:	0.0
Fat (gm):	5.4	Veg.:	0.0
Sat. fat (gm):	1.2	Fruit:	0.0
Cholesterol (mg):	65	Bread:	0.5
Sodium (mg):	164	Meat:	2.5
% Calories from fat:	28	Fat:	0.0

GRILLED ORANGE ROUGHY WITH ASIAN VEGETABLES VINAIGRETTE

Orange roughy is caught off New Zealand. You can substitute Ono, a delicately flavored Pacific fish in the mackerel family.

6 Servings

1¼–1½ lbs. orange roughy fillets, cut into serving portions
½ cup orange juice
2 tablespoons lime juice, freshly squeezed
½ teaspoon fennel seeds
2 oranges, sliced

Asian Vegetables

1 onion, sliced thin
3 cups bok choy, sliced thin
1 can (6½ ozs.) water chestnuts, drained, sliced
½ cup oriental mushrooms, reconstituted, drained, sliced
1½ cups beansprouts
½ cup cilantro, chopped

Vinaigrette

½ cup red wine vinegar
1 tablespoon light soy sauce
2 cloves garlic, minced
½ teaspoon fresh ginger root, grated
¼ teaspoon pepper

Put fish fillets in shallow glass bowl. Separately, mix orange juice, lime juice, and fennel seeds. Pour marinade over fish. Let fish marinate 1 hour.

Arrange orange slices in pairs on prepared grill. Set a fillet on each of the orange slices. Grill, covered, over hot coals 4 to 6 minutes, without turning. Fish will lose translucence and turn opaque when done. Using a long-handled spatula, remove fish to individual plates.

Asian Vegetables and Vinaigrette: Toss all vegetables in salad bowl. Combine all vinaigrette ingredients and toss with Asian vegetables. Serve vegetables with fish.

Nutritional Data

PER SERVING		EXCHANGES	
Calories:	229	Milk:	0.0
Fat (gm):	5.9	Veg.:	3.5
Sat. fat (gm):	0.2	Fruit:	0.5
Cholesterol (mg):	15	Bread:	0.0
Sodium (mg):	155	Meat:	2.0
% Calories from fat:	22	Fat:	0.0

GRILLED WHOLE RED SNAPPER WITH JALAPEÑO MAYONNAISE

Indirect grilling requires that a pan of liquid, usually water, be placed in the grill and surrounded by hot coals. We usually cook with the direct method, that is, grilling over a bed of hot, glowing coals, but not here.

4 Servings

Jalapeño Mayonnaise

- ½ cup fat-free mayonnaise
- ½ cup plain non-fat yogurt
- 2 jalapeño peppers, seeded, chopped (use caution; wear rubber gloves and do not rub your eyes)
- ¼ cup cilantro, minced
- ¼ teaspoon cumin

Red Snapper

- 3–3½ lbs. whole red snapper, cleaned, scaled, with head and tail intact
  Canola oil, or non-stick cooking spray
- 1 hinged fish rack for grill
- 1 lemon, sliced
- 2 tablespoons tarragon wine vinegar
- 1 tablespoon tarragon, or 1 tablespoon fresh tarragon

Jalapeño Mayonnaise: In small bowl, combine mayonnaise, yogurt, peppers, cilantro, and cumin. Taste to adjust seasonings. Cover and refrigerate until needed. Stir before serving.

Red Snapper: Set fish on sprayed fish grill rack. Put lemon slices in fish cavity. Sprinkle fish with tarragon vinegar and tarragon.

Close fish rack. Arrange charcoal for indirect grilling, and place fish in center of grill. Cover grill and cook about 20 minutes, turning once or twice, until fish turns opaque and flakes easily. Remove fish to serving platter, and serve with Jalapeño Mayonnaise.

Nutritional Data

PER SERVING		EXCHANGES	
Calories:	438	Milk:	0.0
Fat (gm):	12.6	Veg.:	0.0
Sat. fat (gm):	3.0	Fruit:	0.0
Cholesterol (mg):	125	Bread:	0.0
Sodium (mg):	393	Meat:	7.0
% Calories from fat:	27	Fat:	1.0

GRILLED RED SNAPPER WITH NACHOS

The nachos help to give this dish a festive flair. This recipe calls for Alpine Lace low-fat cheese because it is very satisfactory and does not have the cholesterol of most other cheeses.

4 Servings

1¼ lbs. red snapper fillets, cut into 4 pieces
1 teaspoon garlic powder
4 bay leaves
 Heavy-duty aluminum foil
24 salt-free nachos
4 tablespoons Alpine Lace low-fat cheese, grated
 Canola oil, non-stick cooking spray

S prinkle fillets with garlic powder, and press 1 bay leaf into the skin of each piece of fish. If bay leaf has trouble sticking to fish, use a few drops of water to help it adhere.

Fold a 24-inch long sheet of heavy-duty aluminum foil in half. Set nachos in center of foil and sprinkle them with cheese. Fold up foil envelope style. With tip of sharp knife, pierce pouch 4 to 6 times for steam vents.

Arrange fillets on sprayed grill rack over hot coals. At the same time, place envelope of nachos on edge of grill away from intense, direct heat.

Grill fish 4 to 5 minutes, turn snapper with long-handled spatula, and continue cooking until done, about 4 minutes longer or to taste. Fish is done when it turns opaque, is just firm to the touch, and will flake easily when prodded with fork.

Transfer fish to plates and serve with nachos. Remind guests to discard bay leaves before eating fish.

Nutritional Data

PER SERVING		EXCHANGES	
Calories:	250	Milk:	0.0
Fat (gm):	8.6	Veg.:	0.0
Sat. fat (gm):	6.1	Fruit:	0.0
Cholesterol (mg):	52	Bread:	0.5
Sodium (mg):	131	Meat:	3.0
% Calories from fat:	30	Fat:	1.0

GRILLED HADDOCK WITH BLUE CHEESE DRESSING AND BROCCOLI

You might wonder how we can use blue cheese in a book dedicated to slimmer recipes? The answer is easy: we use a very small amount of cheese, just enough to give a hint of its delicious, rich flavor.

5 Servings

1¼–1½ lbs. haddock steaks
2 tablespoons sherry
Sage leaves (optional)
½ teaspoon pepper
Canola oil, or non-stick cooking spray
4 green onions, trimmed, leave whole
1 tablespoon blue cheese, crumbled
½ cup plain non-fat yogurt

Steamed Broccoli
4 cups broccoli spears and florets, trimmed
½ teaspoon tarragon
¼ teaspoon pepper

Brush haddock steaks with sherry and press one sage leaf into each steak. Sprinkle with pepper.

Set haddock on sprayed grill rack over hot coals. Grill fish 3 minutes, turn over, using long-handled spatula, and continue cooking until fish is done. The haddock will flake easily and turn opaque. Do not overcook.

At the same time, grill onions, 3 to 4 minutes, turning once. The onions will begin to char.

Transfer fish to serving plate and position onions around fish.

Mix blue cheese into yogurt. Spoon cheese dressing over fish.

Steamed Broccoli: Place on steamer rack over water that has been brought to a boil. Reduce heat, cover steamer, and continue cooking 15 minutes or until broccoli is tender. Drain broccoli and arrange decoratively on fish platter.

Nutritional Data

PER SERVING		EXCHANGES	
Calories:	131	Milk:	0.0
Fat (gm):	1.4	Veg.:	1.0
Sat. fat (gm):	0.4	Fruit:	0.0
Cholesterol (mg):	54	Bread:	0.0
Sodium (mg):	123	Meat:	2.0
% Calories from fat:	10	Fat:	0.0

SMOKED WHITEFISH

It is both creative and fun to add aromatics to the water pan when smoking. For example, when using apple wood, I might add 3 to 4 cinnamon sticks and the peel from 1 orange to the water. The additional flavor is delicate yet flavorful.

8 Servings

3–3½ lbs. whole whitefish, cleaned, scaled, with heads and tails intact
2 green onions, trimmed, leave whole
1 orange, sliced, reserve peel
3 cinnamon sticks
3 pieces plum wood, 3–4 in. long, or mesquite chips, soaked in water 30 minutes, drained

Rinse fish and pat dry. Arrange onions and orange slices in center of fish. Be sure to trim off belly flap, as this is where much of the fat is stored.

Prepare smoker according to manufacturer's directions. Fill water pan three-quarters full of hot water. Add cinnamon sticks and orange peel. When coals are hot and glowing, add drained wood. Replace water pan and grill.

Place whitefish on lowest rack and cover. Smoke fish until done to taste. The whitefish will be opaque and slightly firm to the touch. Skin will turn a slight golden color. It should take about 2½ hours for fish to smoke. Remember, time required for grilling and smoking can only be approximate because of variable factors such as wind, temperature, heat of coals, and distance from heat source.

Using a long-handled spatula, transfer fish to serving dish and cool before serving. When ready to serve, remove and discard skin for ease in eating. If you wish to store fish, wrap it well in foil or plastic wrap because it will have a permeating smoky odor that could be transmitted to other food in refrigerator.

Smoked whitefish is a treat at breakfast with bagels and light cream cheese, at lunch, boned and on a salad, or for a main course at dinner, perhaps with a vegetable-pasta salad.

Nutritional Data

PER SERVING		EXCHANGES	
Calories:	154	Milk:	0.0
Fat (gm):	1.3	Veg.:	0.0
Sat. fat (gm):	0.1	Fruit:	0.0
Cholesterol (mg):	44	Bread:	0.0
Sodium (mg):	69	Meat:	3.0
% Calories from fat:	7	Fat:	0.0

GRILLED CLAMS WITH WHOLE-WHEAT PASTA

Clams and mussels cook alike: directly on grill, in a grill rack, on a bed of seaweed, or in a packet of aluminum foil. As with mussels, discard any clams that do not open after grilling.

4 Servings

- 4 cups whole-wheat pasta, cooked according to package directions
- 2 teaspoons margarine
- 4 cloves garlic, minced
- 4 tablespoons chives, minced
- 1 teaspoon each: basil; oregano
- ¼ teaspoon each: salt; pepper
- 36 little-neck clams, washed

When ready to serve, cook pasta according to package directions and drain. Toss pasta with margarine, garlic, chives, basil, oregano, salt, and pepper. Divide pasta evenly, and place on 4 heated plates.

Put clams directly on grill or use a grill rack. Cover. Clams should be grilled over hot coals 3 to 4 minutes. Discard any unopened clams. Carefully transfer clams onto pasta, allowing clam juices to flow onto pasta. Serve immediately.

Nutritional Data

PER SERVING		EXCHANGES	
Calories:	399	Milk:	0.0
Fat (gm):	4.4	Veg.:	0.0
Sat. fat (gm):	0.5	Fruit:	0.0
Cholesterol (mg):	85	Bread:	2.5
Sodium (mg):	300	Meat:	4.0
% Calories from fat:	10	Fat:	0.0

SMOKED SCALLOPS WITH FRUIT SALSA

Salsa can be prepared the day before serving. Toss and taste the salsa to adjust seasonings at serving time.

6 Servings

Fruit Salsa
(makes about 3 cups)

2 kiwi peeled, chopped
1 mango, peeled, pitted, chopped
1 red Delicious apple, cored, skin left on, chopped
3 tablespoons fresh mint, chopped
¼ cup cilantro or parsley, chopped

Scallops
1¼ lbs. sea scallops
½ cup chili sauce
½ teaspoon chili powder
¼ teaspoon red pepper flakes (optional)
3 cups hickory chips, soaked in water 30 minutes, drained

Fruit Salsa: Combine kiwi, mango, apple, mint, and cilantro in bowl. Cover and refrigerate until serving time. This can be done in advance. Stir salsa before serving.

Scallops: Prepare smoker according to manufacturer's directions. Rinse scallops and pat dry. Mix together the chili sauce, chili powder, and red pepper flakes. Spread seasoning mixture over scallops.

When coals are hot, drain wood chips and sprinkle over coals. Replace grill. Fill water pan three-quarters full of hot water and, using pot holders, return it to smoker.

Place scallops on grill rack over grill. Cover and smoke about 1 hour or until done. Time may vary according to weather, heat, and distance of food from heat source. Scallops are done when they are opaque, light golden color, and just firm to the touch. Check coals and water pan after about 45 minutes to make sure there is enough.

Transfer scallops to individual plates and serve with Fruit Salsa. Good as a first course with Southwestern or Mexican food or as a main dish.

Nutritional Data

PER SERVING		EXCHANGES	
Calories:	140	Milk:	0.0
Fat (gm):	0.9	Veg.:	0.0
Sat. fat (gm):	0.1	Fruit:	0.5
Cholesterol (mg):	25	Bread:	0.0
Sodium (mg):	393	Meat:	2.0
% Calories from fat:	6	Fat:	0.0

GRILLED MEDITERRANEAN SHRIMP

All fish is best just cooked or slightly underdone, and shrimp is no exception. If shrimp is overcooked, it will become rubbery. When shrimp have just lost their translucent quality, they are done.

5 Servings

- 1¼ lbs. extra-large shrimp, shelled, deveined
- ½ cup dry white wine
- ½ teaspoon each: crushed red pepper; oregano; garlic powder
- 1 bunch parsley, chopped
- 1 large onion, minced
  Olive oil, or non-stick cooking spray
- 1 oz. feta cheese (optional)

Place cleaned shrimp in bowl. Cover with wine that has been mixed with crushed red pepper, oregano, and garlic powder. Stir so that all shrimp are touched by flavoring liquid. Let shrimp stand 30 minutes, stirring once.

Meanwhile, mix parsley and onions together. Arrange vegetables on a platter as a bed for the shrimp. Set aside.

Drain shrimp and place them on sprayed grill rack over hot coals. Grill shrimp 2 to 3 minutes on each side or until they are no longer translucent.

Transfer shrimp to prepared serving platter. Sprinkle with crumbled feta cheese. Serve hot.

Nutritional Data

PER SERVING		EXCHANGES	
Calories:	116	Milk:	0.0
Fat (gm):	1.0	Veg.:	0.0
Sat. fat (gm):	0.2	Fruit:	0.0
Cholesterol (mg):	174	Bread:	0.0
Sodium (mg):	201	Meat:	2.0
% Calories from fat:	8	Fat:	0.0

DOWN EAST GRILLED LOBSTER AND CORN

Lobsters from Maine and Nova Scotia are sold live and whole. Sometimes you can find them boiled, but it is best to cook your own. The fresher the better; never buy a dead lobster.
To keep a live lobster at home, store in the refrigerator for one or two days at the most. Seaweed and ice help keep the lobster alive.

4 Servings

- 4 ears fresh corn
- 4 live lobsters, 1¼–1½ lbs. each
- 2 teaspoons margarine, softened at room temperature
- 1 lemon, cut into wedges

Pull back corn husks and remove silk. Replace corn husks. Soak corn in water 30 minutes before grilling. Drain. Set aside.

Prepare lobsters for grilling. Split it lengthwise and remove and discard stomach and intestinal vein.

Place lobsters, shell side up, on a hot grill. Cook 7 to 8 minutes. Turn lobster over and continue cooking 2 minutes or until meat is cooked. The meat will be opaque and will start to separate slightly from shell. As with all seafood, do not overcook lobster.

While you are grilling lobsters, cook corn directly on grill 6 to 9 minutes. Rotate it every 3 minutes. Corn husks will be charred.

Remove lobsters with spatula and serve on individual plates with corn ears. Spread each lobster with margarine (optional) and garnish with lemon wedges.

Nutritional Data

PER SERVING		EXCHANGES	
Calories:	291	Milk:	0.0
Fat (gm):	3.1	Veg.:	0.0
Sat. fat (gm):	0.5	Fruit:	0.0
Cholesterol (mg):	147	Bread:	1.0
Sodium (mg):	811	Meat:	4.0
% Calories from fat:	10	Fat:	0.0

8.
FISH SOUPS

FISH STOCK

Fish stock is one of those wonderful bases or flavorings that you can prepare, pour into an ice cube tray, freeze, and store in a sealed plastic bag in the freezer. Fish bones are usually free if you inquire at your fish counter. Make friends with your fishmonger; he or she is usually most knowledgeable and helpful.

Serves 6

(makes about 1½ quarts (6 cups)

2–3	lbs. fish bones from a non-oily fish such as haddock
	Cheesecloth
1	large onion, roughly chopped
1	stalk celery, sliced
2	bay leaves
7–8	whole black peppercorns
½	teaspoon kosher or sea salt
½	teaspoon white pepper
2	quarts water

Wash fish bones, discarding gills. Cut a double piece of cheesecloth large enough to hold the fish bones. Set bones in the center of cloth, wrap, and seal cloth shut, using kitchen string. Usually bones fall apart during cooking and this helps to make removal easier.

Combine in stockpot, bones, onions, celery, bay leaves, peppercorns, salt, pepper, and water. Bring stock to a boil over high heat. Reduce heat to simmer. Continue simmering stock 30 minutes. It is necessary to skim soup if it gets foamy during cooking.

Discard cheesecloth and bones. Cut a piece of cheesecloth large enough to fit strainer or colander. Set strainer over large bowl and strain stock. Taste and adjust seasonings.

Cool stock. Store stock in jar in refrigerator or pour it into ice cube trays, freeze, remove from trays, and store cubes in sealed plastic bag.

Nutritional Data

PER SERVING		EXCHANGES	
Calories:	17	Milk:	0.0
Fat (gm):	0.1	Veg.:	0.0
Sat. fat (gm):	0.0	Fruit:	0.0
Cholesterol (mg):	11	Bread:	0.0
Sodium (mg):	191	Meat:	0.0
% Calories from fat:	8	Fat:	0.0

SEAFOOD MONGOLIAN HOT POT

*This one-pot meal is cooked at the table by none other than the guests themselves.
The original hot pot had a coal-burning brazier, but we have had success with an electric
wok or frying pan. The pan is placed in the center of the table and filled with hot fish
or chicken stock. Dishes of uncooked fresh fish and vegetables are arranged decoratively on
the table. Each guest adds his or her personal choices of foods. The pot is then covered
and allowed to cook. When cooked, the guests, with the aid of chopsticks or oriental
strainers, retrieve the food--usually not what he or she has put into the hot pot. The
hostess adds some broth to the bowl, with the aid of a ladle. One can offer a side dish of
rice or any number of sauces such as chili, Hoisin, or lemon sauce. Tea is the beverage of
choice to complete the meal.*

6 Servings

6–8 cups Fish Stock (see recipe) or chicken stock
1 lb. fresh or thawed fish fillets, such as haddock, grouper, snapper
½ lb. fresh spinach, trimmed
½ lb. fresh medium-large shrimp, deveined, butterflied
2 cups lettuce, shredded
½ cup bean curd, cut into ½-in. cubes
½ cup green onions, minced
1 can (6½ ozs.) water chestnuts, sliced
½ cup tomatoes, thinly sliced
½ cup green or red bell peppers, seeded, sliced
⅓ cup chili sauce (optional)

When ready to serve, heat fish stock and transfer carefully into electric wok set in center of table. Cut fish into thin slices and arrange it on a plate with spinach. Clean shrimp and place decoratively on plate with shredded lettuce. Set out bean curd, green onions, water chestnuts, tomatoes, and peppers on separate plates.

Offer chopsticks or oriental strainers to each guest. Encourage guests to add their own food. Cover wok and allow to cook on high.

When food has cooked, about 10 minutes, ask guests to remove food and ladle it over soup into their soup bowls. You might want to serve cooked rice or noodles as a side dish. Serve chili sauce to pass at the table.

Nutritional Data

PER SERVING		EXCHANGES	
Calories:	214	Milk:	0.0
Fat (gm):	3.3	Veg.:	3.0
Sat. fat (gm):	0.5	Fruit:	0.0
Cholesterol (mg):	104	Bread:	0.0
Sodium (mg):	335	Meat:	3.0
% Calories from fat:	14	Fat:	0.0

SEAFOOD WON TON SOUP

◆

Won ton wrappers may be purchased at most supermarkets and at oriental food stores. They come in two sizes. If only the larger size is available, simply cut it into four equal parts for won tons. Keep wrappers well covered and refrigerated until needed.

◆

8 Servings

Seafood Filling

⅓ lb. orange roughy fillets
2 green onions, minced
¼ cup broccoli, cooked, cooled, drained, chopped
1 egg white, slightly beaten
½ teaspoon light soy sauce
½ teaspoon ground ginger

Seafood Won Tons

16 won ton wrappers
1 egg white, slightly beaten (use to seal wrappers)
6 cups Fish Stock (see recipe), or chicken stock
1 cup spinach, chopped
¼ teaspoon white pepper
¼ cup parsley, minced

Seafood Filling: First, debone fish fillets. Cut fish into 1-inch pieces and grind. Put ground fish in glass bowl. Mix in onions, broccoli, egg whites, soy sauce, and ginger. Set aside.

Seafood Won Tons: Place a single won ton wrapper, with point facing you, on a table. Put 1 teaspoon of filling in center of each wrapper. Moisten edges of wrapper. Fold opposite corners of won ton together, forming a triangle. Seal edges securely with egg white. Put won tons on a lightly floured plate. Cover with plastic wrap until ready to cook.

Bring fish stock or chicken stock to a boil in large pot. Reduce heat to simmer and add won tons. Stir in spinach, pepper, and parsley. Continue cooking 5 to 7 minutes. Won Tons are done when they are soft and fish is cooked. Serve 2 Won Tons in each bowl of soup. Serve hot.

Nutritional Data

PER SERVING		EXCHANGES	
Calories:	85	Milk:	0.0
Fat (gm):	1.2	Veg.:	0.0
Sat. fat (gm):	0.0	Fruit:	0.0
Cholesterol (mg):	11	Bread:	0.5
Sodium (mg):	223	Meat:	1.0
% Calories from fat:	13	Fat:	0.0

CANTONESE FISH SOUP

This is a light, delicate fish soup that is very easy to make and can be prepared with frozen fish.

4 Servings

4–5 cups Fish Stock (see recipe)
1 lb. haddock fillets, or other firm fish
2 teaspoons dry white wine
2 teaspoons fresh ginger root, minced
3 green onions, minced
½ teaspoon sesame oil (optional)
¼ teaspoon pepper
1 cup spinach, chopped

Pour stock into large saucepan. Cut fish into 1-inch strips; add fish to stock. Mix in wine, ginger root, onions, sesame oil, pepper, and spinach.

Bring soup to a boil; reduce heat to simmer. Continue cooking until soup is hot and fish is cooked, 5 to 10 minutes. Fish is cooked when it is opaque and flakes easily. Taste soup to adjust seasonings.

Ladle soup into individual bowls and serve hot.

Nutritional Data

PER SERVING		EXCHANGES	
Calories:	102	Milk:	0.0
Fat (gm):	0.8	Veg.:	0.0
Sat. fat (gm):	0.1	Fruit:	0.0
Cholesterol (mg):	63	Bread:	0.0
Sodium (mg):	264	Meat:	2.0
% Calories from fat:	8	Fat:	0.0

Magyar Fish Stew with Jellied Fish

It is the Hungarian paprika and the caraway seeds that flavor this interesting soup. The fish can be served in the soup or jellied and served separately, perhaps as a luncheon dish.

---

8 Servings

   2 lbs. bass fillets, reserve bone frame, head, and
     tail for soup stock
   ½ lb. halibut, cut into 8 pieces
   ¼ teaspoon salt
 1½ cups onions, sliced
   3 stalks celery, sliced
   1 teaspoon caraway seeds
   1 tablespoon Hungarian paprika
   1 tomato, sliced
   1 red bell pepper, seeded, sliced
   1 envelope unflavored gelatin
   8 chilled lettuce leaves
   3 hard-boiled egg whites, chopped
   2 tablespoons parsley, minced

S et bones, head, and tail in bottom of soup pot. Add salt, onions, and celery; cover with water. Bring mixture to a boil.

Mix in caraway seeds and paprika. Reduce heat to simmer and continue cooking 45 to 50 minutes. Cool, drain, and discard bones, head, and tail.

Return soup stock to clean pot. Add fish, tomato, and pepper. Simmer, uncovered, 15 to 20 minutes. Gently, with a slotted spoon, stir. Do not let fish break up. Fish is cooked when it turns opaque and is just firm. Remove fish with slotted spoon and place on plate.

There are two ways to enjoy this fish soup. Place a piece of fish in each deep bowl and cover with fish soup. Or serve the soup hot with the fish, as a side dish, chilled and enveloped in gelatin.

To coat fish in gelatin, transfer 2 cups of fish stock to a bowl. Mix in gelatin to dissolve. Heat mixture, stirring constantly. Chill slightly to soft stage, and spoon gelatin over fish, which lies on lettuce leaves. Sprinkle with chopped egg whites and parsley.

Nutritional Data

PER SERVING		EXCHANGES	
Calories:	172	Milk:	0.0
Fat (gm):	3.1	Veg.:	0.5
Sat. fat (gm):	0.7	Fruit:	0.0
Cholesterol (mg):	56	Bread:	0.0
Sodium (mg):	197	Meat:	3.0
% Calories from fat:	17	Fat:	0.0

FISH SOUP (CALDO DE PESCADO)

This is an easy fish soup with an interesting selection of vegetables. It can be changed to accommodate the fish that is available to you. Try using frozen fish in the stew; just defrost in the refrigerator overnight or quickly in the microwave.

10 Servings

1 lb. Pacific rockfish fillets
¾ lb. red snapper, fillets
¾ lb. medium shrimp, peeled, deveined
   Olive oil, or non-stick cooking spray
2 cups onions, chopped
3 cloves garlic, minced
1 large red bell pepper, seeded, chopped
2 cups cooked potatoes, peeled, sliced
3 cups Fish Stock (see recipe)
1 can (28 ozs.) crushed red tomatoes, include
   juice
2 large ears corn, husked, cut into 1-in. rounds,
   trim ends
¼ teaspoon each: grated orange rind; cayenne;
   turmeric

C ut fish and shrimp into 1-inch pieces. Remove with tweezers any bones that may have been left in fish. Set aside.

Spray a stockpot or other large pot with oil. Saute onions, garlic, and peppers about 5 minutes, partially covered, stirring occasionally. Add potatoes, fish stock, tomatoes, and corn. Mix in remaining ingredients. Bring soup to a boil and reduce heat to simmer. Continue cooking 15 to 20 minutes.

Add fish and continue cooking 5 minutes or until fish is cooked. Fish will become opaque and will flake and fall apart easily when done. Ladle soup into deep bowls.

Nutritional Data

PER SERVING		EXCHANGES	
Calories:	211	Milk:	0.0
Fat (gm):	2.7	Veg.:	2.0
Sat. fat (gm):	0.6	Fruit:	0.0
Cholesterol (mg):	99	Bread:	0.0
Sodium (mg):	579	Meat:	3.0
% Calories from fat:	11	Fat:	0.0

SOPA AZTECA

My husband and I recently vacationed in Mexico, where we had a soup similar to this one for lunch.

6 Servings

   Olive oil, or non-stick cooking spray
2 corn tortillas
1 cup red onions, sliced
4 cloves garlic, minced
¾ lb. red snapper fillets, cut into 1-in. pieces
¼ cup avocado, chopped
6 cups Fish Stock (see recipe)
½ teaspoon each: cumin seeds; red pepper flakes
¼ cup cilantro, minced
6 tablespoons low-fat, low-cholesterol, shredded
   Alpine Lace cheese

S pray a non-stick frying pan and saute tortillas about 10 seconds on each side over high heat. Remove from pan and, using a pair of kitchen scissors, cut tortillas into noodle-like thin strips. Set aside.

   Again spray a large saucepan or soup pot and saute onions and garlic over medium heat 5 minutes, partially covered. Stir onions occasionally and cook, until onions are soft, over medium heat. Add remaining ingredients except cheese. Simmer until fish is cooked. Fish will turn opaque and flake easily when done.

   Ladle hot soup into individual bowls and sprinkle with cheese.

Nutritional Data

PER SERVING		EXCHANGES	
Calories:	132	Milk:	0.0
Fat (gm):	2.8	Veg.:	1.0
Sat. fat (gm):	0.4	Fruit:	0.0
Cholesterol (mg):	32	Bread:	0.0
Sodium (mg):	306	Meat:	2.0
% Calories from fat:	19	Fat:	0.0

SKINNY FISH-OF-THE-DAY SOUP

The great fish stews, such as cioppino are really made with the fish that is on hand that day. You realize that fish of similar types can be interchanged easily with good taste results. So with this in mind, here is a skinny fish-of-the-day soup.

8 Servings

1 lb. cod or halibut, or combination, fresh or defrosted, cut into 1-in. pieces

½ lb. red snapper, cut into 1-in. pieces

8 little-neck clams, or cherrystone clams, washed well

½ lb. jumbo shrimp, shelled, deveined, butterflied

Olive oil, or non-stick cooking spray

1 cup onions, chopped

4 cloves garlic, minced

4 large tomatoes, chopped

¼ cup parsley, minced

½ teaspoon each: freshly ground black pepper; oregano; basil

3 bay leaves

½ cup dry white wine

1 cup tomato juice

5 cups Fish Stock (see recipe)

1 slice dry Italian bread, cut into cubes

½ teaspoon garlic powder

Wash and cut fish and shellfish. Set aside.

Spray a soup pot or other large pot with oil. Saute onions and garlic, partially covered, over medium heat about 5 minutes or until onions are soft, stirring occasionally. Add tomatoes, parsley, seasonings, wine, and tomato juice.

Simmer 5 minutes, then add seafood and stock. Continue cooking until fish is cooked; discard any unopened clams. Fish is cooked when it is opaque and flakes easily.

While fish is cooking, prepare croutons. Spray a non-stick frying pan with oil. Cut bread into ½-inch cubes and add to pan. Sprinkle cubes with garlic powder and cook over medium heat, stirring often to prevent burning. Cubes will toast and brown. Remove from heat.

Taste soup to adjust seasonings; discard bay leaves. Ladle soup into deep bowls and sprinkle with croutons. Serve hot.

Nutritional Data

PER SERVING		EXCHANGES	
Calories:	172	Milk:	0.0
Fat (gm):	1.6	Veg.:	1.0
Sat. fat (gm):	0.3	Fruit:	0.0
Cholesterol (mg):	93	Bread:	0.0
Sodium (mg):	366	Meat:	3.0
% Calories from fat:	9	Fat:	0.0

GREEN LIP MUSSEL AND SAFFRON SOUP

Green lip mussels are from New Zealand. Larger in size, they are about 2 inches long and are very tasty.

6 Servings

2 lbs. green lip mussels, well scrubbed
1 onion, sliced
½ cup dry white wine
2 bay leaves
1 carrot, chopped
½ teaspoon thyme
  Pinch of saffron
2 cups bottled clam juice
2 tablespoons cornstarch
2 cups 2% or skim milk

S crub mussels and discard any opened ones. Set aside.
Put onions, wine, bay leaves, carrots, thyme, and saffron in saucepan. Bring mixture to a boil. Reduce heat to medium and add mussels. Cover pan tightly and continue cooking 3 to 5 minutes or until mussels open. Discard any mussels that do not open. Remove mussels from pan, leaving any mussel juice in pan.
Puree vegetable mixture and return to saucepan. Add clam juice. Remove ½ cup of the liquid and mix it with cornstarch; then stir this mixture back into pan. Bring soup to a boil over medium heat, stirring constantly. Soup will thicken slightly.
Return mussels, still in their shells, and add milk. Warm the soup and serve. Discard bay leaves.

Nutritional Data

PER SERVING		EXCHANGES	
Calories:	131	Milk:	0.5
Fat (gm):	2.7	Veg.:	1.0
Sat. fat (gm):	1.0	Fruit:	0.0
Cholesterol (mg):	34	Bread:	0.0
Sodium (mg):	289	Meat:	1.0
% Calories from fat:	19	Fat:	0.0

LINGUINE CLAM SOUP

Remember to buy only the freshest clams available. Buy only clams that are tightly closed, and after cooking discard any that have not opened. There are three types of clams, which are distinguished by their age and size: the little neck clam is named after Little Neck Bay in Long Island. The cherrystone clam is just an older version of the little neck, named after Cherrystone Creek in Virginia. There is a third clam, preferred in chowder—the Quaghaug. It is bigger than the cherrystone and is found along the Atlantic coast.

6 Servings

- 32 fresh little neck or cherrystone clams, washed
- 6 cloves garlic, minced
- 1 cup dry white wine
- 4 cups bottled clam juice
- ¼ teaspoon red pepper flakes, or to taste
- ½ lb. linguine, broken into pieces
- ¼ cup parsley, minced

Put clams, garlic, and wine in large saucepan or soup pot. Bring liquid to a boil over medium-high heat. Cover and continue cooking 4 to 5 minutes or until clams have opened. Discard any unopened clams. Using slotted spoon, remove clams and set aside.

Add clam juice and pepper to remaining broth in saucepan. Simmer soup 4 to 5 minutes until garlic is soft.

Cook linguine according to package directions or until just tender, *al dente.* Drain linguine and divide among soup bowls. Add clams and soup. Sprinkle with parsley. Serve hot.

Nutritional Data

PER SERVING		EXCHANGES	
Calories:	292	Milk:	0.0
Fat (gm):	2.2	Veg.:	0.0
Sat. fat (gm):	0.2	Fruit:	0.0
Cholesterol (mg):	51	Bread:	2.0
Sodium (mg):	284	Meat:	3.0
% Calories from fat:	7	Fat:	0.0

CANADIAN CHOWDER

An easy soup to prepare on one of those busy days, it can be made quickly using defrosted or fresh fish.

6 Servings

Canola oil, or non-stick cooking spray
1 large onion, minced
2 leeks, cleaned, sliced thin
1¼ cups carrots, sliced
1¼ cups celery, sliced
2 cups water
1 lb. cod or halibut, cut into 1-in. pieces
1 can (28 ozs.) crushed tomatoes, include liquid
1 cup 2% or skim milk
½ teaspoon white pepper
¼ teaspoon mace
¼ cup chives, minced

S pray soup pot or saucepan with oil. Saute onions and leeks, partially covered, over medium heat, until soft, stirring occasionally. Add carrots, celery, and water. Continue cooking, partially covered, 15 minutes or until vegetables are tender.

Add fish and tomatoes and cook 5 minutes. Lower heat and stir in milk, pepper, and mace. Simmer only until soup is hot and fish is cooked. Fish is done when it flakes easily and is opaque.

To serve soup, ladle it into individual bowls and sprinkle with minced chives. Serve hot.

Nutritional Data

PER SERVING		EXCHANGES	
Calories:	153	Milk:	0.0
Fat (gm):	1.8	Veg.:	3.0
Sat. fat (gm):	0.7	Fruit:	0.0
Cholesterol (mg):	33	Bread:	0.0
Sodium (mg):	317	Meat:	1.5
% Calories from fat:	10	Fat:	0.0

GUMBO

This classic Southern soup is here updated to a lighter version.

8 Servings

Canola oil, or non-stick cooking spray
1 cup onions, sliced
2 cups okra, sliced
3 cups tomatoes, peeled, seeded
4 cups Fish Stock (see recipe), or chicken stock
1 green bell pepper, seeded, sliced
¼ teaspoon red pepper flakes
¾ lb. red snapper fillets, remove bones
¾ lb. extra-large shrimp, peeled, deveined
1 teaspoon gumbo file powder
2 cups hot, cooked rice

S aute onions and okra in a sprayed pan over medium heat until onions are tender, about 5 minutes, stirring occasionally. Stir in tomatoes and stock. Simmer 5 minutes. Stir in remaining ingredients except rice and file powder.

Simmer 10 minutes or until shrimp and fish are cooked and turn opaque. Discard bay leaves. Remove gumbo from heat and stir in gumbo file powder.

Scoop rice into soup bowls. Ladle hot soup over the rice. Serve hot.

Nutritional Data

PER SERVING		EXCHANGES	
Calories:	189	Milk:	0.0
Fat (gm):	1.5	Veg.:	1.5
Sat. fat (gm):	0.3	Fruit:	0.0
Cholesterol (mg):	86	Bread:	1.0
Sodium (mg):	200	Meat:	1.5
% Calories from fat:	7	Fat:	0.0

9.
FISH SALADS

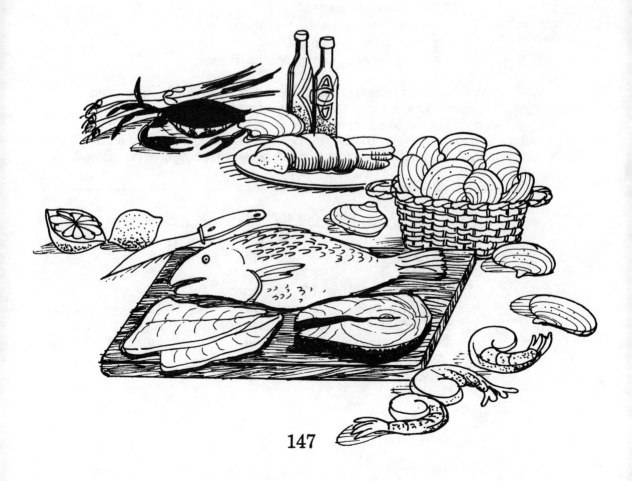

CARIBBEAN TUNA SALAD

Tuna is a most versatile fish. There are many recipes in this book for this wonderfully firm, meaty fish, but the following recipe uses canned tuna. Canned water-packed tuna is always at hand and a fine base for a salad.

4 Servings

Dressing
- ⅓ cup non-fat mayonnaise
- ⅔ cup non-fat vanilla yogurt
- 2 tablespoons golden raisins
- ½ teaspoon ground cinnamon
- ¼ teaspoon ground nutmeg

Tuna Salad
- 1 can (6½ ozs.) water-packed tuna, drained
- 1 cup fresh pineapple chunks
- 1 cup mango, chopped
- 3 cups romaine lettuce, roughly chopped
- ½ cup red onions, thinly sliced
- ¼ teaspoon each: salt; pepper; tarragon

Dressing: Mix together all ingredients in small bowl. Taste to adjust seasonings. Cover and refrigerate until serving time.

Tuna Salad: Flake tuna and put in salad bowl. Mix in pineapple chunks, mango, lettuce, and onions. Season with salt, pepper, and tarragon. Toss salad with Dressing. Spoon into serving bowls. Serve chilled.

Nutritional Data

PER SERVING		EXCHANGES	
Calories:	275	Milk:	0.5
Fat (gm):	8.7	Veg.:	0.5
Sat. fat (gm):	1.7	Fruit:	1.5
Cholesterol (mg):	19	Bread:	0.0
Sodium (mg):	437	Meat:	1.5
% Calories from fat:	28	Fat:	1.0

ULTIMATE GRILLED TUNA SALAD

How many of us grew up on tuna salad sandwiches? Here is the ultimate tuna salad made from fresh tuna grilled to perfection.

4 Servings

Lemon-Orange Marinade

- 1 cup orange juice, freshly squeezed
- 3 tablespoons lemon juice, freshly squeezed
- 1 teaspoon thyme
- ½ teaspoon each: rosemary; thyme
- ¾ lb. tuna steaks, wash and pat dry

Grilled Salad

- Olive oil, or non-stick cooking spray
- 3 cups hickory chips or plum wood, soaked 30 minutes, drained
- 1 tomato, sliced
- 1 green bell pepper, seeded, cut into 1½-in. strips
- 1 red onion, sliced
- 2 tablespoons raspberry vinegar
- 2 cloves garlic, minced
- ¼ teaspoon pepper
- ¼ cup non-fat plain yogurt
- 2 tablespoons non-fat mayonnaise

Lemon-Orange Marinade: Combine all ingredients and pour into plastic bag. Add tuna steaks and seal securely. Turn bag several times so that all sides of fish are touched by marinade. Set bag in shallow dish and let stand 1 hour. Drain tuna.

Grilled Salad: Spray a grill rack. Place tuna and vegetables on rack. When coals are glowing and ashen in color, set drained wood chips over coals. Replace grill. Put rack in place and grill tuna 4 to 5 minutes, turning once, until done to taste. Fish is cooked when it is opaque and flakes easily when prodded with fork.

Cook tomatoes briefly on each side and remove from grill. Grill peppers and onions until just charred on both sides.

Toss, in deep bowl, vinegar, garlic, pepper, yogurt, and mayonnaise. Flake tuna and add to bowl. Cut and add vegetables.

Serve tuna salad on crisp lettuce leaves with warm whole-wheat rolls or bread of your choice.

Nutritional Data

PER SERVING		EXCHANGES	
Calories:	166	Milk:	0.0
Fat (gm):	1.2	Veg.:	1.0
Sat. fat (gm):	0.3	Fruit:	0.5
Cholesterol (mg):	39	Bread:	0.0
Sodium (mg):	143	Meat:	2.0
% Calories from fat:	6	Fat:	0.0

MARINATED SQUID SALAD WITH NACHO CHIPS

Squid can be purchased cleaned and frozen; just defrost in refrigerator, wash, and cut into thin strips. If you buy the squid fresh, first wash and slice. To clean the squid, remove the tentacles and bony beak by squeezing it from the sack; discard the bone. Then discard the skin by peeling it; rinse and slice. My recommendation is to ask your fishmonger to clean them for you.

8 Servings

- 1¾ lbs. fresh squid, cut into ½-in. rings
- 1 cup Mexican beer
- ¼ cup lime juice, freshly squeezed
- 4 cloves garlic, minced
- ⅓ cup green onions, minced
- ½ teaspoon cumin
- ¼ teaspoon red pepper flakes
- ¼ cup cilantro, minced
- 8 blue nacho chips

Blanch cleaned and sliced squid in lightly salted boiling water 1 minute. Rinse squid in cold water. Cool and drain.

To make the marinade, combine beer, lime juice, garlic, onions, cumin, red pepper flakes, and cilantro in a bowl. Put squid in large plastic self-sealing bag. Pour marinade over squid. Seal bag securely. Turn bag several times so that all surfaces of the squid are touched by marinade. Place the bag in a shallow dish and marinate at least 24 hours. Turn bag occasionally during marinating procedure.

To serve the marinated squid in a footed glass, shred a small amount of lettuce and place it in bottom of glass. Spoon marinated squid into glass, and serve 1 blue nacho chip on the side. Serve with cold Mexican beer.

Nutritional Data

PER SERVING		EXCHANGES	
Calories:	102	Milk:	0.0
Fat (gm):	1.7	Veg.:	0.0
Sat. fat (gm):	0.3	Fruit:	0.0
Cholesterol (mg):	185	Bread:	0.0
Sodium (mg):	72	Meat:	2.0
% Calories from fat:	15	Fat:	0.0

MOCK LOBSTER SALAD WITH AVOCADO SAUCE

Mahimahi when cooked is a medium-textured fish, but cold it slightly resembles the taste and texture of lobster. Therefore, it has been nicknamed the "poor man's lobster." Snapper and sea trout are fish that can be substituted for mahimahi.

6 Servings

Light Avocado Sauce
- ¼ medium avocado, peeled
- ¼ cup plain non-fat yogurt
- 2 teaspoons red wine vinegar
- ¼ teaspoon each: hot pepper sauce; salt; tarragon
- ¼ cup cholesterol-and fat-free mayonnaise

Salad
- Canola oil, or non-stick cooking spray
- 1¼–1½ lbs. mahimahi fillets
- 1 tablespoon orange peel, grated
- 4 cups assorted lettuce, Boston, head, romaine, or oak leaf, washed, dried well, torn into bite-sized pieces
- 1 large tomato, sliced thin
- 1 orange, sliced thin
- 1½ cups red onions, thinly sliced

Light Avocado Sauce: In small bowl, mash avocado, discarding stone. Mix in yogurt, vinegar, hot pepper sauce to taste, salt, and tarragon. Add mayonnaise and blend well. Taste to adjust seasonings. Cover and refrigerate until needed.

Salad: Spray frying pan and cook fish 6 to 8 minutes, turning once or twice. Fish is done when it turns opaque and is slightly firm to the touch. Sprinkle fish with orange peel as it cooks. The fish slices better when chilled, so you may cook it the day before and refrigerate covered. Slice fish into thin slices, or cut into chunks, and put in deep bowl. Toss fish with the Avocado Sauce.

Divide and arrange lettuce among 6 salad plates. Spoon mahimahi salad in center of each plate. Arrange tomato and orange slices around salad. Sprinkle salads with thin slices of red onion. Serve chilled.

Nutritional Data

PER SERVING		EXCHANGES	
Calories:	139	Milk:	0.0
Fat (gm):	3.3	Veg.:	1.0
Sat. fat (gm):	0.6	Fruit:	0.0
Cholesterol (mg):	55	Bread:	0.0
Sodium (mg):	296	Meat:	2.0
% Calories from fat:	21	Fat:	0.0

HADDOCK PASTA SALAD WITH SZECHWAN DRESSING

Most recipes that originated in the Szechwan area of China are spicy. The degree of heat depends on you; season to taste. To toast sesame seeds, spread them on a pie plate and toast in a preheated 350° F. oven 5 minutes, stirring once.

6 Servings

Szechwan Dressing

- 3 tablespoons red wine vinegar
- 1 teaspoon honey
- ½ teaspoon chili garlic sauce, available at oriental grocery stores and large supermarkets
- ¾ teaspoon ginger root, grated
- ¼ teaspoon each: salt; Tabasco sauce (more if you desire)
- ½ cup plain non-fat yogurt
- 2 teaspoons toasted sesame seeds

Haddock-Pasta Salad

- 2½ cups cooked haddock or cod, flaked
- 5 green onions, chopped
- 2½ cups broccoli florets, blanched, cooled
- 1 cup beansprouts, blanched, cooled
- 1 cup snow peas, trimmed
- 5 cups cooked pasta shells, drained

Szechwan Dressing: In a small bowl, mix together vinegar, honey, chili sauce, ginger, salt, Tabasco, and yogurt. Taste to adjust seasonings. Cover lightly and refrigerate until serving time.

Toast sesame seeds and set aside.

Haddock-Pasta Salad: Using a large bowl, toss fish with onions, broccoli, beansprouts, snow peas, and pasta. Toss salad with Szechwan Dressing when you are ready to serve. Sprinkle sesame seeds over top of salad.

Bring salad to the table and serve from bowl, or place a lettuce leaf in the center of individual salad plates and spoon on salad. Serve chilled.

Nutritional Data

PER SERVING		EXCHANGES	
Calories:	264	Milk:	0.0
Fat (gm):	1.9	Veg.:	1.5
Sat. fat (gm):	0.2	Fruit:	0.0
Cholesterol (mg):	35	Bread:	2.0
Sodium (mg):	164	Meat:	1.5
% Calories from fat:	7	Fat:	0.0

FISH HASH SALAD

Fish hash is a recipe for left-over, cooked fish. I fondly remember my grandmother making this dish and serving it with horseradish. In preparing this recipe use either defrosted or fresh fish, and serve on a bed of crisp greens.

6 Servings

- 3 cups cooked halibut or cod, flaked (or other fish of your choice)
- 2¼ cups cooked potatoes, cooled, diced
- ¼ cup green onions, minced
- 2 egg whites, slightly beaten
- ¼ teaspoon each: salt; white pepper; celery seeds
  Canola oil, or non-stick cooking spray
- 3 cups lettuce, washed, drained, torn
- ½ cup green onions, chopped
- 2 large tomatoes, sliced thin
- ¼ cup red horseradish
- 1 cup plain non-fat yogurt

I n a large bowl, toss together flaked fish, potatoes, onions, egg whites, and seasonings.

Spray a non-stick frying pan. Cook fish hash over medium-high heat until hot, stirring occasionally. If you like your hash highly seasoned, add a dash of Tabasco sauce or use bacon bits to taste.

To serve, divide lettuce onto plates. Sprinkle with onions and set tomatoes around plates. Spoon hash onto lettuce leaves. Stir horseradish into yogurt and pass it at the table.

Nutritional Data

PER SERVING		EXCHANGES	
Calories:	148	Milk:	0.0
Fat (gm):	1.6	Veg.:	1.0
Sat. fat (gm):	0.3	Fruit:	0.0
Cholesterol (mg):	19	Bread:	0.5
Sodium (mg):	394	Meat:	1.5
% Calories from fat:	10	Fat:	0.0

"CRAB" SALAD WITH TOMATO DRESSING

Surimi, or imitation crab, is available at the fish counter of most supermarkets. It is made using a Japanese process in which fresh fish is processed, flavored, and re-formed into a crablike shape. It is then cooked. Most of the fish used is pollack, a saltwater fish found off the coast of Alaska. Some real crab is also included. Flavorings, preservatives, and stabilizers are added to the fish compound. This product is high in protein and lower in cholesterol and fat than some fish. It does contain sugar and salt.

6 Servings

Tomato Dressing

12	large plum tomatoes, seeded, chopped
⅓	cup onions, chopped
1	tablespoon balsamic vinegar
1	teaspoon best quality olive oil
1	tablespoon honey mustard
1	tablespoon basil
¼	teaspoon pepper

Salad

2	cups surimi (crab substitute), flaked, washed, patted dry
1	cup celery, chopped
2	cups cucumbers, seeded, chopped
2	cups lettuce, roughly chopped

Tomato Dressing: Combine all ingredients in bowl. Taste to adjust seasonings. Cover and refrigerate until needed.

Salad: In a large bowl, toss surimi, celery, cucumbers, and lettuce. Toss Tomato Dressing with salad and serve chilled. Good with crusty bread.

Nutritional Data

PER SERVING		EXCHANGES	
Calories:	112	Milk:	0.0
Fat (gm):	2.2	Veg.:	2.0
Sat. fat (gm):	0.3	Fruit:	0.0
Cholesterol (mg):	7	Bread:	0.0
Sodium (mg):	382	Meat:	1.0
% Calories from fat:	16	Fat:	0.0

JAMBALAYA SHRIMP SALAD

We have adapted jambalaya to use grilled shrimp.

6 Servings

Jambalaya Dressing
- ½ cup plain non-fat yogurt
- ½ cup non-fat mayonnaise
- 2 cloves garlic, minced
- 3 green onions, chopped
- ¼ teaspoon each: oregano; pepper
- ⅛ teaspoon Tabasco, or to taste

Shrimp Salad
- 2 cups shrimp, grilled
- 2 large tomatoes, seeded, chopped
- 1½ cups cooked rice
- 2 teaspoons imitation bacon bits, or to taste

Jambalaya Dressing: In a small bowl, stir together yogurt and mayonnaise. Mix in garlic, onions, oregano, pepper, and Tabasco. Taste to adjust seasonings. Cover and refrigerate until needed.

Shrimp Salad: In a large bowl, toss shrimp with tomatoes, rice, and bacon bits. Toss salad with Jambalaya Dressing. Serve chilled.

Nutritional Data

PER SERVING		EXCHANGES	
Calories:	264	Milk:	0.0
Fat (gm):	7.8	Veg.:	0.0
Sat. fat (gm):	1.6	Fruit:	0.0
Cholesterol (mg):	84	Bread:	2.0
Sodium (mg):	241	Meat:	1.0
% Calories from fat:	27	Fat:	1.5

RED SNAPPER SEVICHE

Seviche is interesting because you do not cook it but simply let the fish marinate in citrus juice until "cooked." It is a good dish for entertaining because it can be prepared days before serving.

---

6 Servings

1 lb. very fresh red snapper fillets
1 cup lime juice, freshly squeezed
1 cup red onions, thinly sliced
½ teaspoon pepper
¼ teaspoon salt
3 cloves garlic, minced
3 bay leaves
1 tablespoon olive oil
2 cups tomatoes, peeled, seeded
3 tablespoons cilantro or parsley, chopped
6 nicely shaped lettuce leaves

C heck fish by running your fingers over surface to see if there are any bones. Remove bones with tweezers. Cut fish into ½–¾-inch pieces. In a ceramic or glass bowl, toss fish with all remaining ingredients except lettuce.

Cover bowl loosely; marinate seviche in refrigerator for at least 48 hours. Toss fish 2 or 3 times a day. Fish is done when it is opaque and firm to the touch. Taste to adjust seasonings.

To serve, mound seviche on pretty lettuce leaves.

Nutritional Data

PER SERVING		EXCHANGES	
Calories:	121	Milk:	0.0
Fat (gm):	3.5	Veg.:	1.0
Sat. fat (gm):	0.6	Fruit:	0.0
Cholesterol (mg):	28	Bread:	0.0
Sodium (mg):	130	Meat:	1.5
% Calories from fat:	26	Fat:	0.5

INDEX

Eat Well & Stay Healthy
with Good Health Books from Surrey

The Free and Equal® Cookbook
by Carole Kruppa

From appetizers to desserts, these 150-plus, *sugar-free* recipes will make your mouth water and your family ask for more! Includes soups, salads, entrees, desserts, snacks—even breakfast treats. Now you can make great dishes like cioppino, Caesar salad, shrimp Louisiana, stuffed peppers, and chicken cacciatore, yet keep control of calories, cholesterol, fat, and sodium. Calorie counts and diabetic exchanges.

The Free and Equal® Dessert Cookbook
by Carole Kruppa

Make cheese cake, black bottom pie, chocolate bon bons, cookies, cakes, and much more *all sugar-free*. More than 160 delicious recipes that help you control calories, cholesterol, and fat. Calorie counts and diabetic exchanges.

The Microwave Diabetes Cookbook
by Betty Marks

More than 130 delicious, time-saving, *low fat, sugar-free* recipes for everyone concerned with heart-health, and especially those with diabetes. Easy-to-follow directions for everything from appetizers to desserts, vichyssoise to pizza. Complete nutritional data, calorie counts, and diabetic exchanges.

Thinner Dinners in Half the Time
by Carole Kruppa

Make your own diet dishes—such as Mediterranean artichoke dip, roast pork chops Calypso, chicken Veronique, and marinated salmon with pasta—then *freeze ahead* to keep your fridge filled with fast fixings. You'll enjoy better taste—and better nutrition—than expensive commercial frozen foods that are usually high in fat and sodium. Over 160 delicious time-savers. Complete nutritional data, including calories per serving and diabetic exchanges.

The Restaurant Companion: A Guide to Healthier Eating Out
by Hope S. Warshaw, M.M.Sc., R.D.

All the practical information you need to order low-fat, high-nutrition meals in 15 popular cuisines! At Chinese, Italian, or Mexican restaurants (plus many others), fast-food chains, salad bars—even on airlines—you'll *learn how to stay in control* of calories, fat, sodium, and cholesterol when eating out.

The Love Your Heart Low Cholesterol Cookbook, Revised Second Edition
by Carole Kruppa

Give your taste buds a treat and your heart a break with 250 low-cholesterol recipes for everything from appetizers to desserts. Enjoy the great tastes—with *no cholesterol*—of deviled eggs, Italian bean soup, oriental chicken salad, chocolate cake, and many more easy-to-make delights. Nutritional data, diabetic exchanges, and calorie counts.

The Love Your Heart Mediterranean Low Cholesterol Cookbook
by Carole Kruppa

Hearty, exotic, traditional, delicious—all great words to describe these mouth-watering dishes from the south of France, Italy, Spain, Greece—even Morocco. Yet the 200-plus recipes—from appetizers to desserts—are *streamlined for heart health.* Keeping the tempting, sun-drenched flavors while controlling fat, cholesterol, sodium, and calories is this book's genius! Complete nutritional data and diabetic exchanges.

Feeding Your Baby From Conception to Age 2
by Louise Lambert-Lagacé

First U.S. edition. Complete information on good nutrition for babies—and mothers—before, during, and after pregnancy. Includes breast-feeding (with tips for working moms), dealing with problem eaters, recipes for baby food. *Extensive nutritional information in plain talk.*

"Skinny" Recipes for Low-Fat Meals

Skinny Beef
by Marlys Bielunski

Over 100 healthy, *low-fat recipes* for America's favorite entree. The first major beef cookbook to follow American Heart Association guidelines of 30% or fewer calories from fat. The great tastes of beef in all its varieties: stir-frys, salads, barbecues, roasts, and easy-to-make 30-minute meals that combine beef with other ingredients for delicious entrees. Nutritional data for each recipe.

Skinny Pizzas
by Barbara Grunes

Our national fun food now qualifies as our *national good-health food, too!* These 100-plus tempting, easy, economical recipes trim away excess fat, cholesterol, and calories so you can serve pizza without guilt. Includes: shrimp, spinach, chicken, teriyaki, stir-fry, vegetarian, Creole, scallop, Szechwan, cheesecake pizzas and dozens more. Plus 18 pizzas for the barbecue. *Follows AHA guidelines* of 30% or fewer calories from fat. Nutritional data for each recipe.

Skinny Seafood
by Barbara Grunes

The sea's bounty affords happy, healthy eating—especially when it's prepared to increase natural flavor while controlling fat, cholesterol, and calories. These 101 creative recipes range from steamed lake trout and grilled snapper to seafood pizza, finnan haddie, scallop burritos, whole Maine lobster, Cajun catfish, Cantonese fish soup, jambalaya, shrimp salad—even a Wisconsin fish boil! *Follows AHA guidelines* of 30% or fewer calories from fat. Complete nutritional data.

Skinny Soups
by Ruth Glick and Nancy Baggett

More than 100 delicious, hearty yet calorie-wise soups from elegant crab and mushroom bisque, exotic Malaysian chicken scallion, and unusual Italian garden to standbys such as French onion, chicken-rice, and New England fish chowder. *Recipes keep calories from fat under 30%*, and emphasize low sodium, low cholesterol, and high-fiber ingredients. Complete nutritional data.

Skinny Spices
by Erica Levy Klein

50 nifty homemade spice blends, ranging from curries and herb blends to chilis and Moroccan mint, to make even diet meals exciting! Spice blends require no cooking and add *zero fat, cholesterol, or calories* to food. Includes 100 recipes that use the blends.

Skinny Cakes, Cookies, and Sweets
by Sue Spitler

It *is* possible to create over 100 low-fat desserts and sweets, *none exceeding 250 calories per serving*—not even the cheesecakes! Sue Spitler proves it with carrot cake, baked Alaska, apple pie, caramel flan, oatmeal cookies, plums in port, chocolate cake, and 90 more marvelous treats slimmed down to AHA guidelines of 30% or fewer calories from fat. Easy to prepare—delicious. Nutrition data for each recipe.